INTRA-DAY TRADING TACTICS

Greg Capra

Marketplace Books
Glenelg, Maryland

This book, along with other books, is available at discounts that make it realistic to provide them as gifts to your customers, clients, and staff. For more information on these long lasting, cost effective premiums, please call us at 800-272-2855 or e-mail us at sales@traderslibrary.com.

ISBN: 1-59280-314-8
ISBN 13: 978-1-59280-314-9
Printed in the United States of America.

Table of Contents
Intra-Day
Trading Tactics

PUBLISHER'S PREFACE

What you have in your hands is more than just a book. A map is simply a picture of a journey, but the value of this book extends well beyond its pages. The beauty of today's technology is that when you own a book like this one, you own a full educational experience. Along with this book's author and all of our partners, we are constantly seeking new information on how to apply these techniques to the real world. The fruit of this labor is what you have in this educational package; usable information for today's markets. Watch the video, take the tests, and access the charts—FREE. Use this book with the online resources to take full advantage of what you have before you.

If you are serious about learning the ins and outs of trading, you've probably spent a lot of money attending lectures and trade shows. After all the travel, effort, expense, and jet lag, you then have to assimilate a host of often complex theories and strategies. After thinking back on what you heard at your last lecture, perhaps you find yourself wishing you had the opportunity to ask a question about some terminology, or dig deeper into a concept.

You're not alone. Most attendees get bits and pieces out of a long and expensive lineage of lectures, with critical details hopefully sketched out in pages of scribbled notes. For those gifted with photographic memories, the visual lecture may be fine; but for most of us, the combination of the written word and a visual demonstration that can be accessed at will is the golden ticket to the mastery of any subject.

Marketplace Books wants to give you that golden ticket. For over 15 years, our ultimate goal has been to present traders with the most straightforward, practical information they can use for success in the marketplace.

Let's face it, mastering trading takes time and dedication. Learning to read charts, pick out indicators, and recognize patterns is just the beginning. The truth is, the depth of your skills and your comprehension of this profession will determine the outcome of your financial future in the marketplace.

This interactive educational package is specifically designed to give you the edge you need to master this particular strategy and, ultimately, to create the financial future you desire.

To discover more profitable strategies and tools presented in this series, visit www.traderslibrary.com/TLEcorner.

As always, we wish you the greatest success.

Chris Myers
President and Owner
Marketplace Books

HOW TO USE THIS BOOK

The material presented in this guide book and online video presentation will teach you profitable trading strategies personally presented by Greg Capra. The whole, in this case, is truly much greater than the sum of the parts. You will reap the most benefit from this multimedia learning experience if you do the following.

Watch the Online Video

The online video at www.traderslibary.com/TLEcorner brings you right into Capra's session, which has helped traders all over the world apply his powerful information to their portfolios. Accessing the video is easy; just log on to www.traderslibrary.com/TLEcorner, click *Intra-Day Trading Tactics* by Greg Capra under the video header, and click to watch. If this is your first time at the Education Corner, you may be asked to create a username and password. But, it is all free and will be used when you take the self-tests at the end of each chapter. The great thing about the online video is that you can log on and watch the instructor again and again to absorb his every concept.

Read the Guide Book

Dig deeper into Capra's tactics and tools as this guide book expands upon Capra's video session. Self-test questions, a glossary, and key points help ground you in this knowledge for real-world application.

Take the Online Exams

After watching the video and reading the book, test your knowledge with FREE online exams. Track your exam results and access supplemental materials for this and other guide books at www.traderslibrary.com/TLEcorner.

Go Make Money

Now that you have identified the concepts and strategies that work best with your trading style, your personality, and your current portfolio, you know what to do—go make money!

Meet Greg Capra

Greg Capra is president and CEO of Pristine Capital Holdings, Inc., the nation's leading educational service for self-directed traders. He has 15 years of experience as a day trader and swing trader. Many years ago, Capra realized how to collect valuable intra-day information from stock quotes and store them into an orderly computerized system. He utilized a program called SuperTic to track and evaluate this information, which led him to his pursuit of intra-day trading tactics.

In those days, free online stock charts and quotes were not widely available, and institutional traders had a great advantage over the individual trader. Today, the playing field is more level. Capra saw an opportunity to build an educational and research firm for self-directed, independent traders. This meant that ordinary people could now possess a sophisticated level of research on par with institutional traders and hedge funds.

Capra developed The Pristine Swing Trader, an advisory newsletter with over 60,000 subscribers, and is co-author of the book, *Tools and Tactics for the Master Day Trader* (McGraw-Hill, 2000). Pristine.com was founded in 1994 and combines publication-based education with seminars and education services aimed at helping traders gain an intuitive understanding of the markets. Over 400 seminars are conducted each year around the world.

Before founding Pristine, Capra spent 15 years running his own business. Since founding Pristine.com, his desire has been to educate the individual investor in quantitative analysis of market movements.

Introduction
The Fine Art of Intra-Day Trading

Successful intra-day trading is a fine art—and Greg Capra is a master of the game. With many years of experience in short-term trading strategies, he shares the secrets of intra-day trading in this course book, providing you with a thorough explanation of this high-intensity trading arena.

His theories are based on an understanding of both the markets and the individual trader. While great emphasis is usually placed on stock price movements, chart patterns, and anticipation of pending price direction, Capra also realizes that traders need to develop specific attributes in order to succeed. He believes the three characteristics of winning traders are: confidence, discipline, and patience.

Capra employs a methodical approach, which shows you how pooling an array of indicators can create a single and profitable protocol that you can utilize to make dynamic trades, again and again. His key points include six important levels:

1. There are three fundamental forms of intra-day trading.
2. Intra-day trading involves many psychological demands.
3. There are specific circumstances in which you should trade for wealth or for income.
4. Chart analysis provides insights, notably when you watch 5-minute and 15-minute patterns.
5. Volatility patterns impact your trading choices.
6. The tick indicator is a key timing tool.

Capra's comprehensive course book covers all of the essential elements you need to succeed as an intra-day trader. These include interpretation of moving averages, establishing risk limits through relative strength analysis, and targeting small but consistent gains with minimum risk exposure.

INTRA-DAY TRADING TACTICS

Chapter 1

The Basics: A Smart Starting Point

I have noticed that many options traders create short-term profits by moving in and out of positions, using options for swing trading, and going through the usual set-up signals to move money around. Options are very effective for short-term trading because they require less capital and less risk for the same returns. If you are trading options in this manner, I can assure you that my intra-day strategies will vastly improve your profitability.

> Intra-day trading is specifically designed to create short-term profits by observing price patterns and timing your entry and exit points. It is not magic, just common sense.

If you are not using options and define yourself as a typical long-position equity investor, the system I will show you here will prove to be quite valuable. There is nothing wrong with building a portfolio full of value investments; but, at the same time, you can augment the usual dividends and capital gains with short-term profits. Typically, investors think of stock trading in terms of the trading day. But have you ever wondered why some stocks open at a different level than they closed the day before?

It is not just the fact that so much happens between trading hours that matters. The fact is, the way that price movement occurs at the beginning and end of the day (as well as where prices open) all signal important information. If you learn how to track these indicators, you can create consistent short-term profits to make your portfolio more than the usual decades-long plan to build wealth. You can build wealth over a period of weeks, days, hours, and even minutes.

> No method can produce 100% profits. There are no "sure things" in the market. Risk is ever present, but with my time-proven intra-day trading strategies, you can vastly improve your percentages and, as a result, your level of profits.

Before going on, however, I want to be sure that you know there are always risks involved with day trading and swing trading. The purpose of analyzing tendencies in price is not to provide you with a 100% guaranty; anyone making that claim is not providing you with a realistic promise. The methods I will explain are designed to improve your performance odds.

If you can beat the market half the time, in theory, you will break even. Assuming you place the same amount of capital at risk for every trade, half will win and half will lose. Many investors are fortunate just to achieve a point where they break even, and I think that is dismal. The purpose of my systems is to improve your percentages enough so that you will consistently beat the market, meaning your percentages of good outcomes will improve. You will still have losses, but your profits will outnumber those losses. That is the goal.

I will cover four major points in this book: an introduction to trading; key concept to technical analysis; foundational information for making trades; and putting it all together to make profits.

This chapter deals with introductory topics: styles of trading, definitions, and psychological requirements. My company, Pristine, has broken down trading into four distinct styles. This is useful because it helps you to determine what your own style is and where you fit on the spectrum. It is also important to start out by carefully defining exactly what day trading is, so that we are talking about the same thing. Finally, I will examine the psychological requirements for this type of trading.

Not everyone is well suited to the day trading world, and you need to make sure you are comfortable with the pace of the action, required knowledge level, need for analysis, and the risks involved. My experience tells me that if you are not psychologically suited for day trading, you will not be happy with it; that means the effort will not be worth the trouble. Even if you can make profits from day trading, you need to feel confident and safe with the whole concept for it to work. Going beyond that, you also need to be able to process a lot of information quickly to make timely decisions. If you are not well suited to this, you are probably going to lose money. That defeats your purpose, which is to make money.

> Day trading is a realm of quick action. As part of your overall approach, you will need to be able to process information quickly and make decisions as soon as opportunities come up. Fast action equals profit.

My teaching method is very visual. I will begin with a foundation, simplify the technical aspects of strategies, and demonstrate them with candlestick charts. The charts are central to all of the discussions to follow, so I will explain them in some detail when I first introduce them in graphic form. There is a lot of information to absorb, and you should not expect to take it all in at once. Follow my step-by-step method and, by the end of this book, you will have all of the information you need.

When I began looking into trading systems many years ago, I realized that there are several available. I have read all the books I could find on technical trading, and I realized that, in print, it becomes very complex and difficult to decipher. There is simply so much to remember. So, my goal became specific: I wanted to simplify and get down to the basics, so that it all made sense to someone seeing it for the first time. The tools I use include candlestick charts and moving averages. I will show you how to read and interpret these visual outcomes, in a way that is quite different than anything you have seen or read in the past.

The Visual Tools

As I have said, I like to combine candlestick charts with moving averages. I know that as a starting point, I am going to need to expand on these visual tools and explain them in context for you. These are the primary visual aids you will need.

 See these visual aids in the accompanying video, online at www.traderslibrary.com/TLECorner.

Beyond these, I also am going to explain the Pristine buy and sell setup signals, which are derived from very specific trading patterns you will see on candlesticks and in the moving averages. I base all of my trades around these setup signals, and they serve an important function. Instead of relying on instinct alone (like many traders) I employ a very methodical and precise setup to time my decisions. I will show you how these setups work and how you can duplicate what I have learned to do.

The setup is key; but, moving beyond that, I will also reveal how to interpret price movement using multiple timeframes. For example, your entry point might be based on a short timeframe signal, but the longer timeframe conflicts. In cases like this, going with the longer timeframe usually makes more sense; that is where the power is, and where you can gain some valuable insights in timing your trades. You will see how this works later in the book.

When people are first introduced to candlesticks, it can be very confusing; however, you only need to know about six candlestick patterns. In the interest of keeping everything simple, I will limit my explanation to these six patterns. You do not need to learn everything about candlesticks to succeed with intra-day trading.

> The more indicators you use, the greater the chance for conflicting signals. Going with longer timeframe indicators usually makes the most sense.

The same rule applies to moving averages. I will simply explain how to read and interpret them, and show how you can anticipate entry and exit points. The important thing to remember concerning moving averages is that they foreshadow the key decision points very specifically. I'll show you how this occurs with great regularity, so that your timing will be vastly improved.

> Effective trading systems have to be basic and simple, or you won't have the ability to act quickly. An indicator should reveal a specific bit of information and show you what to do when you see it.

While I will be explaining some highly technical concepts, I will move methodically through them in context. For example, I will demonstrate how retracement levels and Fibonacci patterns work, not as esoteric and technical concepts, but as useable tools for timing your trades. A lot of academic books and articles delve into these advanced concepts on a complex level, but this provides nothing of value to the trader who wants to know, "What does it show, and what should I do when I see it?"

I will also provide you with an analysis of some of the basic technical concepts, such as support and resistance levels. For many people who understand these concepts as they are usually applied, my use of support and resistance is quite different. I use these specifically to anticipate entry and exit points for trades; in other words, the market timing decisions you make can be confirmed and made more accurate when you study the technical aspects of price movement in context.

The five tools, in summary, are:

1. Candlestick charts

2. Moving averages

3. Buy and sell setup signals

4. Retracement level analysis

5. Support and resistance analysis.

These five concepts used in coordination provide you with a powerful trading methodology. Your intra-day decisions will be better timed and you will have more confidence when you use all five of these tools. This system also helps to keep your decisions on an objective level and to avoid the gut reaction pitfall so many traders experience. Most important of all, you have to act quickly in a fast-moving market. The combination of these five tools helps you to make fast and accurate decisions in a matter of mere moments. This system is designed to eliminate the guesswork and improve your timing and, ultimately, your profits.

The Four Types of Trading

The starting point to entering the world of intra-day trading is to identify the kind of trader you are and, perhaps, to decide whether you should be a different type than you have been in the past. There are four types of trading styles: Core, Swing, Guerrilla, and Day Trading. These fall into the two categories of wealth and income.

> A fact overlooked by many people is that you do not always have to take action. If you're not sure about what to do in a particular situation, you should probably stay on the sidelines until the picture clears up.

Remember, this definition phase for the types of trading is designed to help you pick the type you're best suited for and to provide you with alternatives. To master intra-day trading, you begin with this phase and then put it together with the key concepts. I believe that you should never have to determine what you should be doing based on action in the market; you should already know. If everything I cover in this book does not tell you exactly what you should be doing in a particular situation, that means you should stay on the sidelines and do nothing, at least until things become clearer.

This is most important. Many people fail to consider that taking no action—staying on the sidelines—can at times be the smartest strategy of all. If you are uncertain about a strategy or its timing, or if charts and moving averages do not provide a specific setup for you, then taking an action would be a simple guess. The purpose in developing a detailed method such as this is to remove the guess-work from your trading program.

All of the trading styles we discussed earlier have one thing in common: they are all technically based. By this, I mean the sole purpose of these styles is to track a stock's price movement, with the use of technical indicators for decision-making. As a day trad-

FIGURE 1.1 · **Two broad trading categories**

Wealth Trading Styles	**Income Trading Styles**
Core Trading	Guerrilla Trading™
• Weekly Charts • Weeks to Months	• Daily, 60 Min. & 30 Min. • Hours to Days
Swing Trading	Day Trading
• Daily Charts • Days to Weeks	• 5, 15 & 60-Min. • Minutes to Hours

er, you have much more information available than just the price by itself, and all of these styles are based on the technical approach.

Figure 1.1 divides the four types into two broad classifications: wealth styles and income styles.

There are two broad classifications here, wealth and income. These two style divisions define how you approach intra-day trading, so it is critical to study these in line with your own point of view, risk tolerance, and opinions.

Swing and core trading requires that you ignore what's happening in very short timeframes, and that's what most people find very difficult. With all the new, different platforms that are out there and information that you have access to on intra-day trading – especially online –most people start out looking at daily charts. From there, discovering intra-day charts is a logical next step, but then you'll see several different trends that appear to be in conflict with each other.

I will show you how to combine these pieces of information. However, if you end up operating as a core trader or a swing trader, this coordination of different information sources is going to be less valid. Core traders focus on weekly and monthly timeframes, so their charts are much greater in nature than income traders' charts. Swing traders tend to focus on a limited numbers of days, usually three to five and, at the most, will study charts limited to a few weeks' duration.

These chart durations mirror the typical holding periods for wealth traders. In comparison, income trading involves a much shorter duration. With guerilla trading, you would be looking at daily, 60-, and 30-minute charts, and your holding period would to be hours to days. Day trading involves even shorter timeframes, 5-, 15-, and 60-minute charts, and involves holding periods mostly limited between minutes and hours.

> The kind of chart you study defines the kind of trader you are meant to be. Intra-day trading focuses on extremely short timeframes, as small as five minutes.

Clearly, the distinctions between wealth and income trading are substantial in terms of the kinds of charts each side studies as well as the typical holding periods. The styles are vastly different, so you cannot simply assume that all trading is going to be the same. Within the technically-based trading world, there are many different styles, risk levels, and philosophies about what works and what individual traders want to do.

Defining Intra-Day Trading

Most people have heard of day trading and swing trading. The typical day trader moves in and out of positions within a single trading day so that a position that opened in the morning would normally be closed before the end of trading. A swing trader rides the short-term price waves in a three- to five-day period, and bases

FIGURE 1.2- What is Intra-day Trading?

1. A style that covers a holding period of **several minutes to hours.**

2. Three forms of Intra-day Trading: **Scalping Momentum Day**

3. This style of trading has become **widely accepted recently.**

4. Day Traders use **5- & 15-Min. charts** to make entries and exits.

5. Day Trading is best used on **active**, highly **liquid** stocks.

6. Day Traders try to capture smaller gains with **minimal dollar risk.**

7. Day Trading is a style of trading that **May not be suitable for ALL!!**

trades on some very specific buy and sell setup signals. Intra-day trading is quite different than both day and swing trading.

Figure 1.2 summarizes seven important points to remember about intra-day trading and defines it in terms of holding period, types, charts, risk levels, and suitability.

The first point is the style of intra-day trading. It involves a holding period for open positions for a matter of mere minutes to the possibility of several hours. As a variation on day trading, an important distinction is that positions are likely to be left open from one trading day to another; in comparison, day trading usually is defined as opening and closing of positions within a single trading day.

The second distinction involves form, which comes in three varieties. Scalping used to be popular when trading occurred in segments of eighths of a dollar. After decimalization, trading occured with increments as small as one penny, meaning that scalping is really not applicable any more. In those pre-decimalization days, scalpers would bid for stocks and offer shares out to make a profit on the spread. The bigger the position, the better the dollar value of even a very small fractional spread. With commissions and taxes in play, scalping is extremely marginal and, considering the risk, not a very feasible form of intra-day trading.

Momentum trading is more prevalent today among very active traders. As the market begins moving in one direction, momentum traders accept offers. This includes bidding for stocks and turning them over based on the direction of momentum. This continues until the momentum stalls and begins trending in the opposite direction. The momentum trader will then take the opposite position and play momentum in the other direction. This type of trader would be long on the uptrend and short on the downtrend.

> Momentum trading forms the basis of day trading. It involves riding the waves of a trend, either upward or downward, until the signals tell you the wave is ending. Then you reverse and ride the opposite wave.

Pristine day trading style means we will be looking at multiple timeframes, what's happening within the market, and at some market indicators to give us market direction. Our style is less active than the other two styles. It really is more of a thought process. You will now start going through a method of sitting down and doing some analysis about what's happening in a particular stock and what's happening in the market. You will be combining these concepts to make your decisions.

 Get help making those decisions from Capra himself, in the online video at www.traderslibrary.com/TLECorner.

Day trading continues to be popular today because so much can happen to a price from one trading day to another. Many traders simply don't want to leave positions open overnight, including a high volume of trading activity among institutions and hedge funds, in addition to individuals. Intra-day and day trading have become widely accepted in recent years; only a few years ago, day trading was considered a high-risk and fringe form of trading.

The Pristine style of trading combines momentum and day philosophies. We like to use 5- and 15- minute charts for finding entry points, focusing on highly liquid stocks. When you start looking at daily charts, you may see predictable patterns emerging at specific times and under certain conditions. These are things that swing traders look for, the short-term uptrend and downtrend occurring with price and volume setup patterns. But with intra-day trading, our focus is on a much shorter timeframe than the three- to five-day swing trading pattern. The typical swing trading pattern lacks the kind of extremely short-term liquidity we prefer. This simply means that when you buy shares, you have to have a ready market of buyers when you want to sell. And when you're ready to buy, you need a broad range of sellers so you can get your price. Liquidity. That's the key.

However, liquid stocks can move against you rapidly, so intra-day trading relies on institutions and active traders. These are the intra-day trader's trading partners. We only hope, naturally, that our timing is perfect and their timing is wrong. Fortunately, this is often the case. The combination of active trading and highly liquid stocks is the best market for intra-day trading. This narrows the field while presenting your best opportunities for very short-term profits.

Those who act as intra-day traders like to make fantastic percentage gains on small dollar amounts with regularity—rather than hoping for bigger dollar gains with more money. Those dollar changes can also be losses.

The sixth important point is to create situations with minimal dollar risk. Day traders typically are going to be capturing small gains with minimum dollar risk; an underlying premise of intra-day trading is based on this idea as well. We look for situations with low risk and potentially quick profit.

A final important point to make in defining intra-day trading is that it is not going to be suitable for everyone, as a style of trading. Just because you have the ability to sit down in front of a monitor and trade doesn't mean that you have the personality or the risk tolerance to go through the time that it takes to focus on the market all day long. It can be very stressful and it may not be what you want to do. Some people want to invest in high-quality, well-managed value investments, knowing their money will grow slowly and steadily over many years. This is not a profile of an intra-day trading candidate.

The psychological trading requirements you need to succeed in intra-day trading represent the last point to cover in this chapter. I have heard it said that "psychology is 80 to 90%" of effective intra-day trading. It's going to take confidence, patience, and discipline. But how are you going to put all of that together?

First, you will need to remove the subjective analysis, or reduce it, or eliminate it where you can. There seems to be an endless supply of technical indicators out there today with different settings and measurements that you can change the parameters on. As criteria for simply timing a trade, there is also an abundance of information. Typically, a trader goes on a quest of trying to find the ultimate indicator, that foolproof method for perfectly timing every trade, combining different analysis tools that guarantee they're never going to lose money. Well, that's never going to happen; so, you have to eliminate those subjective complexities. Start focusing on where the action is—with the price action and what price trends reveal. Because all of the technical indicators are based on price, my approach is to focus on what's happening within the prices and not on indicators. We will use some simple tools to do just that.

Even with this simplified approach—focusing on price rather than the indicators based on price—the method has to be systematic; you need a means of interpretation just to know what you should be doing, whether it's taking positions or waiting for entry points. This, in turn, is going to build a thought process that will improve your confidence.

It is not just the mechanical process that defines intra-day trading success. The thought process behind it builds confidence, and this is essential if you plan to succeed.

The patience and discipline, once you have the method, will become your job. I can't stop you from pressing the button because you think the price of a stock is moving or because you think that you should be entering or exiting a stock at that very moment. You must apply patience and discipline to your research to find those entry points.

The entire process of moving money in and out of positions is based on these principles; this cannot be stressed too much. There is an old saying that "the market rewards patience" and that is true. Many traders who want to get into the action but don't really understand

A lack of discipline invariably leads to losses and not to profits. If you expect to make a profit, you have to be well-disciplined and resist temptation.

how or why prices move as they do, tend to jump in impulsively, rather than (a) defining the right entry point; (b) investing when the setup develops; and (c) getting out when the other setup, the sell setup, appears. You need to do all of these things to become effective in intra-day trading.

Discipline is crucial because it ensures that you will follow the "rules." People tend to get greedy when they enter positions, and the profits begin to accumulate. Rather than heeding the closing setup, they convince themselves that by holding on for a little longer, they can make even more money. Most of the time, lack of discipline leads to losses and rarely builds in more profits.

In the next chapter, I will explain the foundation of intra-day trading, the three powerful tools you need to succeed. These are charting tools, moving average, and buy/sell setups.

Self-test questions

1. Candlestick charts are best used:

   a. to identify overpriced stocks, at which times the body of the candlestick becomes elongated.

   b. in conjunction with moving averages.

   c. as confirmation of value-investing entry decisions.

   d. only for stocks with very low trading volume.

2. In addition to candlesticks, intra-day traders need:

   a. buy and sell setup signals.

   b. support and resistance analysis.

   c. retracement level analysis.

   d. all of the above.

3. Intra-day trading is defined as:

   a. wealth and income styles, sub-divided into swing and core styles, and guerilla and day styles.

   b. activity strictly limited to single-day trades.

   c. trading involving only 15-minute open positions, regardless of price movement.

   d. the opposite of swing trading.

4. Intra-day trading:

    a. includes holding periods from several minutes to hours.
    b. takes three forms: scalping, momentum, and day.
    c. is based on 5- and 15-minute charts.
    d. all of the above.

5. Successful intra-day trading depends on:

    a. technical experience and advanced training.
    b. patience and discipline.
    c. in-depth study of a company's fundamentals.
    d. all of the above.

For answers, go to www.traderslibrary.com/TLEcorner

Chapter 2

Foundation: The Strong Base for a Profitable Structure

To build a foundation, you need the right tools. In the foundation of intra-day trading, you are going to need charts, moving averages, and setups. This chapter describes these in detail and provides examples of what they reveal and how you can use them. The basic tools for the intra-day trader are summarized in Figure 2-1.

The Trading Tools

The first of these tools is the price and volume chart. Intra-day trading, using the Pristine method, depends on 5-minute, 15-minute, and 60-minute charts. In addition, the charts are always shown in candlestick format, which is necessary in order to quickly spot the direction and duration of price movement. I also like color-

FIGURE 2.1 - Tools of the Pristine Day Trader

Charting Tools: 5-, 15- & 60-Min. Intra-day charts displayed in Candlestick form.
Color coded volume.

Technical Tools: 20- & 200-period 'simple' moving averages.

A Price Pattern: The Pristine Buy & Sell Setup.

coded volume because that enables me to instantly spot changes in typical volume levels.

There are many moving average systems out there, but all you really need are 20-period and 200-period simple moving averages. I don't think weighted averages provide us with any valuable information and can even distort the true picture. So, exponential and other weighting methods simply don't add any value to the analysis. In fact, moving averages are not really signals themselves, but flags. They signal the timing of a decision. For example, when a moving average crosses a price line, that often works as a signal that it is clearly time to take action, either on the buy side or sell side, depending on direction.

Candlestick charts provide immediate, efficient price information and are always used for intra-day trading using the Pristine method.

FIGURE 2.2 -Intra- day Charting

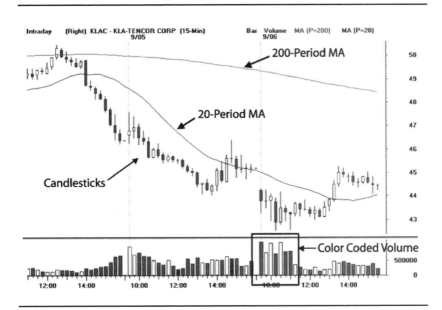

15- MIN. Chart
For color charts go to www. traderslibrary.com/TLEcorner

The price pattern provides you with a basic action plan and the indicators about when to buy and sell. This idea is at the heart of virtually every day trading and swing trading system, but the Pristine method has fine-tuned the setup so that you can proceed with more confidence than with any other type of analysis.

I want to now demonstrate how all of this comes together. Figure 2.2 is a 15-minute chart for Kla-Tencor Corporation (KLAC).

This 15-minute chart is in candlestick form. Before getting into the details, a valuable bit of advice: as an intra-day trader, you may want to put a clock on your monitor to display the time throughout the day. Many traders make the mistake of forgetting about time and, consequently, make assumptions about the outcome of the current candle. This applies to all time frames whether it's the 15-minute or 5-minute charts. Remember, what this distinction means is that the chart entries are separated by the time increment; so, this 15-minute chart should show price levels at 15-minute intervals.

Add a clock to your monitor screen to track short-term intra-day trades and avoid missing out on key entry or exit points. Many traders lose money because they forget to track the time.

Without that regular clock counting the minutes and seconds intra-day to track the end of the time frame being viewed, you can easily assume that the current candle will look the same when it is done as it looked while it was forming, which is typically not the case.

For example, the current candle while forming might signal to you that you should take action, but there are two minutes remaining on that current chart increment. Consider this, as the current candle is forming, its message is a bullish one and you take a position. Once that candle has completed, and its message is now a bearish signal, how are you going to manage that position? You have now entered into a position that you would not have if you had waited for the completion of the time frame.

This scenario is typically what setups what is known as the "impulse trade." A trader sees a signal setting up, but fears the opportunity will be missed, so they enter prior to gaining complete information that was detailed as part of their trading plan. Later, when reviewing the day's trades in the absence of the open market, many traders in that moment asks themselves, what was it that I saw that made me take that trade? Sound familiar?

 Don't let yourself be one of those traders—find out how at www.traderslibrary.com/TLECorner.

In setting up the 20-period and 200-period moving averages, show your moving average lines with distinct colors. By maintaining consistancy in color for each of the averages, you will not get them mixed up in different time periods. You will always know, for example, that the blue line is always the 20-period and the red line is always the 200-period moving average.

You only need these two moving averages. They should be unweighted simple averages; you do not need to complicate the analysis with other period lines. These work best in conjunction with one another and with the candlestick charting.

I also recommend color-coding volume. This helps you to identify buying and selling volume trends quickly. You will usually see higher levels of volume going into candles that are closing up. Selling pressure increases the selling volume, of course, and color-coding helps you to spot this immediately, and to equate the volume trend with what the price reveals on the candlestick. The purpose of color coding moving averages and volume is to be able to immediately see precisely what is happening in the trend at this very moment.

> You can quickly see who is winning the price war with candlesticks. White or lightly-colored bars means the bulls are winning; black means the bears are winning.

The easiest part of the analysis using candlesticks is to see who is winning the price war battle. And, it is the most important and most powerful information you will gain. The value to candlesticks is that you can immediately distinguish between up and down-trending days by the color of the body (that's the rectangular center of the candlestick), which also represents the difference between opening and closing prices for the day. When the trend moves upward, the candlestick's body is lighter; when it closes lower, the candlestick's body is black.

In the case of KLAC, you can see how the different moving average trends have evolved during the time period. The 20-period MA tracks above the actual price levels for most of the time; and because the average covers a smaller number of periods, you expect it to track closely like this. The 200-period MA remains consistently a few points above the current trading action. Later, you will see why this is significant in determining entry points for intra-day trades.

Candlestick Charts

Before going forward, I want to go through a brief lesson on candlestick charts. The various sizes and shapes of the entries are the strongest and most valuable indicators of what is going on; and, once you master the few important points about candlesticks, you will see a vast improvement in your ability to identify price trends the instant you view a chart.

FIGURE 2.3 - The battle between bulls and bears

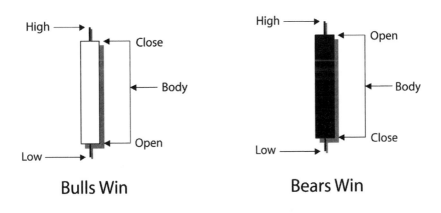

Determining Who Won The Battle
For color charts go to www. traderslibrary.com/TLEcorner

A period's entry is a summary of who won the battle for that period (whether a day or an entry of 15 minutes). In this battle between the bulls and bears, you have two basic outcomes. When a price rises, the bulls win; when a price falls, the bears win. The features of the candlestick summarize everything you need to know about changes in price, as shown in Figure 2.3.

> There is a distinction between the candlestick body (defining open and close) and extent of the upper and lower shadows (defining the period's trading range).

The body of the candlestick (the rectangular portion) represents the trading range for the period between the opening and closing price. When the bulls win, the price rises during the day, so the "open" is at the bottom of the body and the "close" is at its top. On such days, the candlestick is white or light-colored. When the bears win, the body is black; the "open" is at the top while the "close" is at the bottom. On these days, the candlestick's body is black.

Trading is not usually restricted to prices between open and close. For this reason, the candlestick also shows an upper and lower shadow. The range between the top of the upper shadow and the bottom of the lower shadow represents the day's high and low prices.

The size and shape of the body, and the length of the shadow on either side, all reveal important information you need to time entries and exits in your trades. When you begin to overlay candlestick patterns into the context of a trend, those patterns become very powerful. While you can gain the same types of information

FIGURE 2.4 - Six Candle Concepts

• Changing of the Guard™ - COG	All give traders the Same Message
• Wide Range Body - WRB	
• Narrow Range Body – NR	The probability of the current trend changing is increasing.
• Narrowing Range Bodies - NRB	
• Topping Tail - TT	A high probability opportunity may exist to trade.
• Bottoming Tail - BT	

without candlesticks, it is much easier to visualize when used in this format. In today's Internet environment, it is instant and automatic to get highly detailed candlesticks, as well as moving averages, completely calculated, revealed instantly, and color-coded to your specifications.

The major candlestick indicators you need to know include six specific patterns summarized in Figure 2.4.

Changing of the guard, or COG, encompasses many different patterns informing us about the potential for change. The wide range body, or WRB, is a powerful concept because it often tells us we should hold a trade for a longer period of time than we would normally; it can also tell us when momentum might be about to stall.

A narrow range, or NR, and its multiples, NRBs, topping tail and bottoming tail all give us the same message: the probability that the current trend is changing. That is all we are really interested in. We are looking for change and trying to anticipate when it is going to occur. This gives us the ability to either enter or exit a position at the right moment, rather than seeing in hindsight how we lost an opportunity.

> Setup signals work in all kinds of trading environments. They are not unique to a particular style of trading, but to the price patterns they reveal.

When you know what to look for in candlestick patterns, it is not that complex. There is too much hype around the use of candlesticks. In of themselves, they are not a method of trading. Simply, what we are looking for is increasing or slowing momentum and reversals. Candles take various shapes to display this; and, we use them in combination with each other and the other concepts that will be discussed here to determine if there is a high probability that a profitable trade is developing. The bottom line is that there is a point where we can make money, and our approach is to do that where there is a high probability of profit with low risk of loss.

To frame this information in terms of how setups actually work, I want to summarize four important facts for you. These facts are listed in Figure 2.5.

These four facts are simple but profound. First, a setup can be traded in all timeframes. It doesn't matter whether you are operating as a swing or core trader or an intra-day trader; the message of the setup will always be the same.

Second, the setup is a set of bars that occurs in a detailed formation. This pattern establishes extremely short-term uptrends and downtrends and also demonstrates growing strength or weakness when compared to previous trend direction.

Third, this combination of bars is a segment or smaller part of the overall pattern. This is often overlooked by traders. No short-term movement in price should ever be viewed in isolation, but as the latest information in a larger, longer-term pattern. (That longer term might be two hours instead of five minutes, but the point is that no isolated series can be taken as significant until it is put in perspective.) The point is that we are focused on details, and we are trying to remove subjectivity from the analysis.

Fourth, the setup offers a high probability with low risk, which ultimately is what we are looking for: better profits, lower losses. We want to enter trades when we have a minimal dollar risk.

Basic Patterns and Setup Signals

Figure 2.6 shows an example of how the buy and sell setup appears.

The setups are not complicated. The basic pattern has an easily identifiable number of attributes. We typically look for three to five bars in a trend of one direction, and we do not want to see these bars moving more than about 20% into the prior bar's range; the overlap indicates less predictability, and congestion equals uncertainty. We prefer clear, trend movements.

> A setup develops in a predictable manner, but it is not complete until you find the reversal candle, which is the final and essential part of the multi-period setup.

On the left is the basic downtrend pattern. A downtrend is characterized by three to five bars with progressively lower lows and progressively lower highs. At the end of the downtrend, we are likely to see a narrow range day (a more compressed body in the candlestick) with an upper shadow and, often, little or no lower shadow. That is a buy setup.

FIGURE 2.6 - The Pristine Buy and Sell Setup

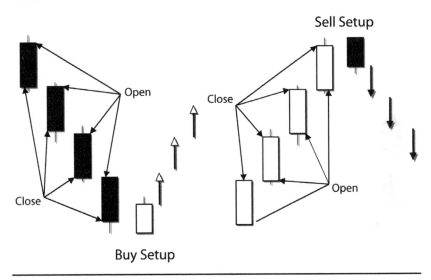

Each new bar opens in the area of the prior bar's close and also closes below its opening price until a reversal of that occurs. The setup is complete after a reversal candle has formed.

For color charts go to www. traderslibrary.com/TLEcorner

On the right is the uptrend, which is characterized by three to five bars with progressively higher highs and higher lows and again with 20% or less overlap between candlestick bodies between days. The uptrend ends with the sell setup, a narrow range day with little or no upper shadow.

The setup is not complete until we see a reversal candle. Next, we have to put these short-term patterns in the context of a trend, which I will explain at the end of this chapter.

FIGURE 2.7 - The Pristine Buy and Sell Setup

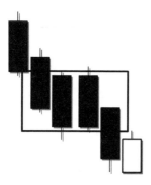
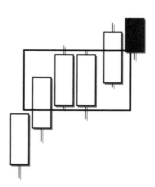

This is NOT what we are looking for!
These bars overlap each other and do not have the predictability we are looking for.

In looking for the entry and exit setup, you also want to be aware of a pattern that is less predictable. Figure 2.7 is an example of what I mean.

It is just as important to know what you do not want to see as it is to recognize what you do want to see. When progressive bars overlap each other, so that one day's bar is in the same range as the previous day's by more than 20%, it is not ideal and more than 50-60% will be forming an area of congestion; so, the trend is uncertain. Price movement is choppy and conflicted; you cannot be

FIGURE 2.8 · Price pattern recognition

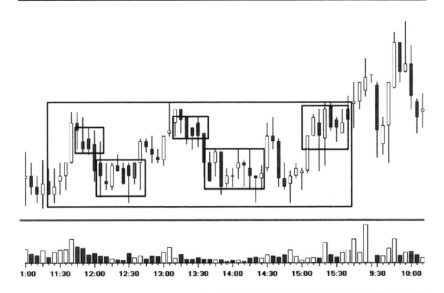

1:00 11:30 12:00 12:30 13:00 13:30 14:00 14:30 15:00 15:30 9:30 10:00

For color charts go to www. traderslibrary.com/TLEcorner

sure whether the trend is going to continue or reverse. The signal is unclear, so you cannot take action with the degree of confidence you need. That 20%—and I mean the real body and not the shadows—is a strong warning signal to watch for.

Let's look at a more extended congestion pattern. Figure 2.8 reveals a series of overlapping bars in a four-hour portion of a single trading day.

Congestion patterns are whippy, unpredictable, and recognized by overlapping candles. What you are seeing here is multiple failures

You do not always have to take action. When the pattern shows price congestion, implying uncertainty, the smart money waits on the sidelines until a clear trend emerges.

in both directions. By this, I mean that the pattern fails to move decisively upward or downward. You see bars in the same trading range of each other. Trying to trade in these congestion patterns is a no-win situation.

The congestion occurs because the markets are uncertain. Uncertainty is one of the three dominating emotions on the market, so these patterns are not appropriate times for you to make a move. The other two emotions—greed and fear—cause prices to overreact to any and all news, and that is where you get the real advan-

---

FIGURE 2.9 - Simple Moving Averages

- Long positions are favored when prices are Above their **20-MA** on a **60-Min.** chart. Entry points are found on **5- or 15-Min.** charts.

- Short positions are favored when prices are Below their **20-MA** on a **60-Min.** chart. Entry points are found on **5- or 15-Min** charts.

- Short positions are considered when prices are extended Above the **20-MA** on a **60-Min**. but Below their **20-MA** on the **5-Min**. chart.

- Long positions are considered when prices are extended Below the **20-MA** on a **60-Min**. but Above their **20-MA** on the **5-Min.** chart.

---

tage. By trading patterns instead of emotions, intra-day trading is a self-disciplined system for getting those short-term profits while avoiding the more common overreactions in the market.

The greed and fear patterns are pretty easy to identify, and that is where our setup signals serve us well. Uncertainty is more difficult because, at times, it can just seem to go on and on; this is where your patience is rewarded. Resist the urge to do anything in the market. Wait out periods of congestion, and you will eventually see either the bulls or the bears win the moment. Then, track the more dependable setup patterns to take advantage of market price movement.

 Learn how to deal with the uncertainty; watch the online video at www.traderslibrary.com/TLECorner.

Moving Average Guidelines

The last portion of this chapter is a series of moving average guidelines. Remember, a moving average (MA) is just that, the average of a specific number of periods. So a 20-period MA is the average of the last 20 periods, and a 200-period MA is the average of the last 200 periods. The number of periods are added up and then divided by the number of periods. These are powerful tracking tools because they even out the chaotic short-term changes in price and show the trend line. With the combination of moving averages and candlestick charts, you have exactly what you need to track price and to seek effective intra-day trading setups.

FIGURE 2.10 - Long Term Intra-Day

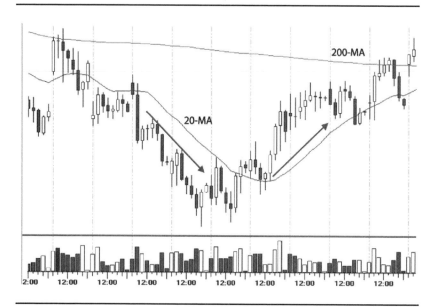

200-MA

20-MA

2:00   12:00   12:00   12:00   12:00   12:00   12:00   12:00   12:00   12:00

60 MIN. Chart
When Prices decline below the 20-MA, favor Short Trades.
When Prices rise above the 20-MA, favor Long Trades.

For color charts go to www. traderslibrary.com/TLEcorner

Here is a look at the indications you receive from simple moving averages. Figure 2.9 provides four basic rules I like to observe in my analysis.

The first guideline involves long positions. These will be favored when prices are above their 20 period MA on a 60-minute chart. We are going to find our entry points on our 5- or 15-minute charts. We want to see that our longer timeframe is moving up. The general rule is that shorter timeframes are stronger entry points.

FIGURE 2.11 - 60-min chart, 5-min chart

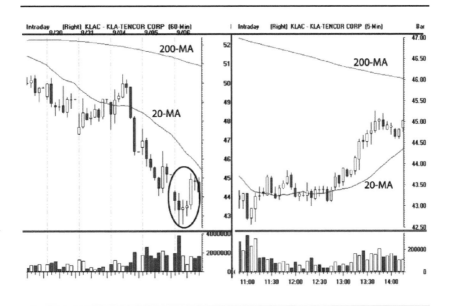

The power is to the downside on the first segment of this chart. When prices begin to rise above the 20 period MA, we will be looking for long trades on our shorter time period.

Short positions are favored when prices are below their 20 period MA on a 60-minute chart, and entry points will be found on 5- or 15-minute charts. The same rule applies for short positions; however, the prices are found on the other side of the 20 period MA.

You gain a lot of insight by observing where price is moving in relation to the 20-period MA. Whether you are long or short, this proximity anticipates action points.

There are times when we may go against the prevailing trend at high probability points, but we'll consider short positions if prices are extended above the 20 period MA on a 60-minute chart; however, we want to see that momentum has slowed. We're going to look for the trend to short below, once the prices have moved under the 20 period MA on a 5-minute chart.

Finally, long positions will be considered when prices are extended below the 20 period MA on a 60-minute chart, but above a 20 period MA on a 5-minute chart. That way, it keeps us from guessing if things are going to turn around. We have allowed the momentum to slow. Once they move above that 20 period MA on a 5-minute chart, we know there has been enough stabilization at that point. This is a more aggressive approach, but these guidelines enable us to take advantage of the moving average-based patterns.

Now, we will see how these guidelines work on an actual chart. Figure 2.10 is a 60-minute chart that combines moving averages with candlesticks.

Figure 2.11 summarizes what we use for long-term analysis with 20 and 200 period moving averages. When prices are declining, the trend favors the short side. The power is to the downside on the first segment of this chart. When prices begin to rise above the 20 period MA, we will be looking for long trades on our shorter time period

These charts show the price moving away from the 20 period MA. The area that we will focus on is in the period when this kind of gap develops. When the price and the 20 period MA begin moving back toward one another, just like at the end of the 5-minute chart's trend, it is a sign that the price is starting to stabilize; this is where a signal arises. As we move into the candlestick concepts in the next chapter, you will see how to interpret this trend.

 Use the online video to nail down your understanding of this signal—watch now at www.traderslibrary.com/TLECorner.

Self-test questions

1. The best charts for intra-day trading are:

   a. 20-period charts limited to single days.

   b. 20-period charts extending over two trading days.

   c. 5-, 15-, and 60-minute charts.

   d. daily charts only.

2. The only moving average systems you need are:

   a. 20 and 200 period simple moving averages.

   b. exponential and other weighted moving average systems.

   c. 5 and 20 period MAs without weighting.

   d. weighted 200 period MAs updated regularly.

3. The candlestick consists of:

   a. a rectangular real body representing the distance between the period's open and close.

   b. color coding for upward or downward movement.

   c. upper and lower shadows representing the period's trading range.

   d. all of the above.

4. Downtrends are characterized by bars with progressively:

    a. lower lows and higher highs.

    b. lower lows and lower highs.

    c. higher lows and higher highs.

    d. higher lows and lower highs.

5. A reversal candlestick tends to have:

    a. an extended real body.

    b. a narrow range.

    c. a very extended high/low range on a short body.

    d. a real body extended 20% or more into the range of the previous day's candlestick.

For answers, go to www.traderslibrary.com/TLEcorner

Chapter 3
Candlestick Concepts: Reading Between the Lines

Candlestick charts are the visual base of our intra-day trading strategy. I want you to succeed in this endeavor, but to do so you need to use candlesticks. They are not difficult to master and, by the end of this chapter, you should be comfortable with them. Their power is that, in a single glance, these charts tell you everything you need to know: price trend, strength, setup signals, both past and evolving and, of course, perspective of the trend with moving averages in mind.

Ask yourself this question: what does the current candle tell you about the prevailing trend? Remembering that you are looking at an intra-day trend, you want to find three to five bars that are moving in the same direction; once you see that, you monitor for the reversal signal, knowing that you are going to act quickly. As you combine your different candlestick concepts, you will see that the movement of price, as expressed in this visual form, will either confirm or contradict what you are observing. Both forms of information are critically important.

> The candlestick is a visual aid to help you quickly and accurately find and identify the trend, and to find reversal signals to help you make decisions in a timely manner.

So now you are ready with your Pristine buy setup and have entered a position. Referring back to the indicated color coding, we will assume you saw three to five red (down or black) bars and then a narrow range green (up or white) bar. The buy setup is there. What is the next bar you are looking for? Another green bar. You should assume that, after the buy setup, the stock's price will to begin climbing. If the next one is a big long red bar to the downside, what are you thinking? Get out. Something's wrong. So, it becomes even more important for you to keep your focus on what is happening on a bar by bar basis.

Is the candlestick trend confirming, or are you questioning what's happening? If you do question your own strategy, ultimately it becomes very difficult for you to lose a lot of money. You should face the fact that any technical system is designed not to provide you with a foolproof money-making plan, but to improve your odds and increase the frequency of profitable and timely decisions. The only way you can really lose a lot of money, if you follow all of the advice I am giving you, is to do one of two things: either you

FIGURE 3.1 - Candlestick Concepts

- Ask yourself, "What does the current candle tell you about the prevailing trend?" Note: A trend = 3-5 bars moving in the same direction.

- Each candle will give us information that either confirms or contradicts that trend.

- Long or Expanding range candles tell us volatility is high or momentum is increasing.

- Short or Narrowing range candles tell us volatility is low or momentum is decreasing.

put your head in the sand and ignore what's happening in the actual price trend, or apply little or no money management into your strategy. Putting it another way, if you ignore the premise and get greedy, putting too much money into a single trade, you will eventually make a poorly timed decision and lose big.

I would now like to teach you four important concepts worth remembering, which can be seen in Figure 3.1.

First, ask yourself what the current candlestick trend reveals about the prevailing trend. (Remember, the "trend" consists of three to five bars moving in the same direction.) Second, remember that each and every entry in the trend either confirms or contradicts the indicated direction. In an uptrend, confirmation occurs when another up candle appears; contradiction occurs when a down candle appears instead. Third, long or expanded range candles tell you that volatility or momentum is on the rise. And fourth, short or narrowing range candles tell you the opposite, that volatility and momentum are decreasing.

> Long real bodies in candlesticks reveal volatility and momentum; and, narrow real bodies reveal a decrease in these important attributes. Remember these points, and finding entry and exit points will be much easier.

All information is valuable. The length of each period's open-to-close range is so significant that it should be continually monitored. The trend itself is only the first indicator; when you see the size of the real body growing or shrinking, you need to be aware of what that means in anticipating price direction.

Contradiction is important for another reason. In the previous chapter, I showed you how congestion patterns evolve and express uncertainty. Remember, the three emotions at work in the market are greed, panic, and uncertainty. The last one is the most troubling because you really do not know what to expect next; you have to wait it out. When you enter a position on a buy setup, what should you do if the trend does not develop as you expect? A period of congestion can follow a short-term trend just as easily as a reversal, and, when a price gets congested, you do not know what will happen next. That is why you want to manage your capital and not put too much into any single trade. These entry setups are not 100%

FIGURE 3.2 - Changing of the Guard Bar- COG

Bullish COGs

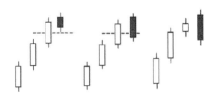

Bearish COGs

- A Bullish COG is defined as three or more consecutive red bars followed by a green bar.
- A Bearish COG is defined as three or more consecutive green bars followed by a red bar.

Tip: While there are different variations, the message is always the same! A reversal in momentum has occurred!

For color charts go to www. traderslibrary.com/TLEcorner

guaranteed; therefore, when you keep dollar levels relatively low, you are managing risk.

I like to describe trend changes as a "changing of the guard" or COG. I've mentioned this previously, but now I will show you what this means in the candlestick chart and in terms of how momentum develops. Figure 3.2 shows you how bullish and bearish COGs evolve.

A COG, can also be termed "the end of the trend," or the point where we expect to see price reverse and begin moving in the opposite direction. The "guard" in this case is either the bulls or the bears, and the point being described by COG is when one side replaces the other.

A bullish COG occurs when you see three or more down bars followed by an up bar. A bearish trend takes place when the directions are reversed. Remember, though, that this COG is going to take place in an infinite number of variations, but the message is always the same: a reversal in momentum has occurred.

Look at the bullish and bearish examples to see what this means. Remember, a downtrend is seen when there are three or more bars with progressively lower lows ands lower highs, and an uptrend is characterized by three or more bars showing higher highs and higher lows. At the same time, watch out for congestion, which is signaled by a bar covering more than 20% of the same territory seen in the previous bar. Congestion changes everything and cancels out the trend. It means that momentum is lost to both sides, at least for the moment.

> Uptrends and downtrends are fairly easy to spot; what might be more subtle is congestion, a period when neither bulls or bears are in control and when the next direction is difficult to find.

When you study candlesticks, you soon realize that the range of open-to-close, or the trading range itself, is also an important forecasting indicator. When you see longer expanding range candles, it means volatility is high, or the momentum is increasing. Short or narrow range candles tell you that volatility is low and momentum is decreasing. When you make this observation within the context of a trend, the messages are going to become very clear.

The end of the trend is strongly indicated when you see narrowing range bars, or NRBs. Figure 3.3 illustrates this trend.

When the difference between high and low begins to narrow over a series, that is a significant trend. Remember the distinction between high-to-low and open-to-close. The high-to-low extends

FIGURE 3.3 - Narrowing Range Bars- NRB

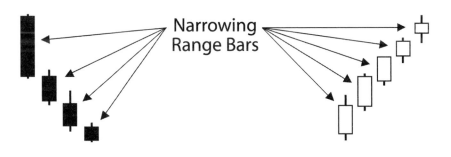

A series of bars in which the difference between the highs and lows is Narrowing. Pristine Tip: While there are different variations, the message is always the same! A slowing in momentum is occurring!

For color charts go to www. traderslibrary.com/TLEcorner

from the tips of the upper and lower shadows for the period, and that is what we are concerned with here. Momentum is slowing when the trading range narrows between high and low for the period; and, while the variations and circumstances are varied, the message is always the same.

That message, concerning momentum, is that the range of price differences between buyers and sellers is closing in, or getting smaller. The narrowing range, NR, means momentum is slowing down, and it is quite likely that momentum is going to shift and the price will begin to move in the opposite direction.

 Hear this message, and more, in the online video at www.traderslibrary.com/TLECorner.

In comparison to narrowing range bars, the narrow range body, or NRB, sends you the same message but in a different way. The pattern is shown in Figure 3.4.

In this formation of a candlestick, the body of the candle is small relative to the overall length of the candle and there may be tails on either side. These candles are often overlooked because, for the most part, traders are looking for ideal candle patterns that suggest a change in direction. However, these NR bodies are telling you the same thing: momentum is slowing. This often leads to a change in direction; but, it is most important at the end of an established trend, following a series of candles. For example, if you were short on the stock and you saw a price pattern developing intra-day on a 5-minute chart, meaning the stock is moving down,

FIGURE 3.4 - Narrow Range Bodies- NR

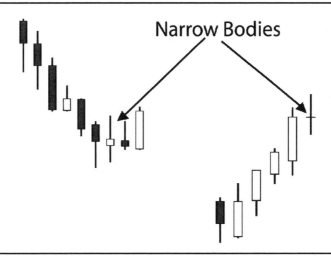

Bars in which the body of the candle is small relative to the overall length of the candle.They may have Tails on either side of the body.

Tip: While there are different variations, the message is always the same! A slowing in momentum has occurred!

For color charts go to www. traderslibrary.com/TLEcorner

you would realize that momentum was slowing here—the time has arrived to take action. You might want to be prudent and take half of your money off the table. That is wise because the trend could reverse, which is what the NR body formation tells you. It gives you a cautionary signal. As long as you are aware of these potential changes, you will stay in touch with what the market is telling you.

The next concept is that of the topping tail bar, or TT. This is shown in Figure 3.5.

FIGURE 3.5 - Topping Tail Bars- TT

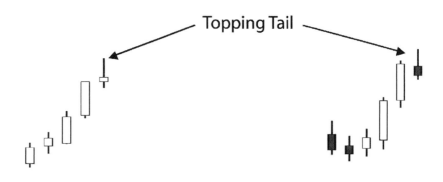

Topping Tail

Bars in which prices had been higher, then supply forced prices lower into the lower part of the bars range.

Tip: While there are different variations, the message is always the same! Distribution has occurred!

For color charts go to www. traderslibrary.com/TLEcorner

A topping tail occurs when bars have moved progressively higher, but the supply of shares is forcing prices lower. The "tail" (upper shadow) is exceptionally long to the upside. This clearly shows that distribution has begun, meaning there is more selling than buying. It signals the end of the run-up. In these bars, prices were higher on the period, but supply has forced those prices down and into the lower segment of the bar's range.

This pattern is a good example of what candles show you, which is what other traders are thinking. In this case, those traders who

FIGURE 3.6 - Candlestick Concepts- Bottoming Tail Bars

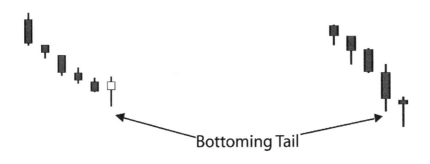

Bottoming Tail

Bars in which prices had been lower, then demand forced prices higher into the upper part of the bars range.

Tip: While there are different variations, the message is always the same! Accumulation has occurred!

bought this stock at the high are now holding loss positions. If you have entered a long position on a setup at the bottom of this trend, the topping tail bar tells you it is time to get out. And, as is the case with all patterns, there may be any number of variations, but the message is always the same. With the topping tail, distribution has taken place and the uptrend may be over.

> Unusually long shadows (tails) imply distribution on the upside; the topping tail anticipates a change in the trend and helps you to pick the entry point more accurately.

FIGURE 3.7 -Wide Range Bar- WRB

- A Bar in which the Candle Body is relatively wide compared to the most recent bars.
- A Wide Range Bar after a period low volatility ignites momentum in that direction
- A Wide Range Bar after an extended advance or decline typically happens near the end of a move. An NR or NRB will signal the turn.

For color charts go to www. traderslibrary.com/TLEcorner

The same rule applies in a downtrend. The bottoming tail bar is illustrated in Figure 3.6.

In this pattern, a downtrend has taken place over a period of days, but now demand has forced the price into the upper segment of the bar's range. The three- to five-day downtrend ends with the bottoming tail. Prices were lower at the end of the bottoming tail, but now accumulation has started and a change is underway. The downtrend is over as buyers begin to take control. You will see many variations of this pattern, but the message is always the same. In this case, sell the short or buy the long.

The bottom tail is exactly opposite of the top, in terms of what it reveals. An unusually long lower shadow (tail) reveals that accumulation has begun and the downtrend is ending.

A wide range bar, or WRB, is a bar in which the candle body is relatively wide compared to the most recent, preceding bars. This longer range, after a time of low volatility, ignites momentum in the direction of the day's price. So a WRB with a downward movement ignites downward momentum. A WRB occurring after an extended advance or decline typically signals the end of the trend and the beginning of a turn. These concepts are shown in Figure 3.7.

If you have not entered a position when you see the WRB, meaning you are seeking an entry point, this will be it; the signal is especially strong. Remember, a lot of traders have been heard to ask, "I gave up my position too soon. How do I hold on for a longer period of time?" When I see a candle like this that's igniting momentum, I know it is time to get in, and if I am already in a position, I am not giving up my shares. I am holding on because this pattern is telling me to hold on for a bigger gain.

A wide range bar taking place after an extended advance or decline typically happens near the end of a move, so the momentum has increased. As the range expands, it means that everybody is jumping on board in that direction. It is typically followed by one of our other candle patterns, suggesting things are going to start moving in the other direction. It is time to make a contrarian decision and go against the crowd, based on what the pattern reveals.

As you start to study intra-day charts, you will spot some interesting things. For example, a candle like this shows up as price starts to accelerate to the downside, and all of a sudden it gets very quiet. Then, 10 or 15 minutes later, the price comes racing back to the upside. When you see this pattern and you are already short, take note of it. The reversal can take place rather quickly, and you can end up giving back a very nice profit very fast.

Next, I want to cover some of the changing of the guard (COG) patterns. Figure 3.8 shows patterns with a narrow body, narrow range bar, wide range bar, and highlights points where COGs appear.

The primary point to be made in this chart is that specific patterns demonstrate slowing or gathering momentum and a switch between bulls and bears at specific times. By knowing how to recognize the changes, you can anticipate momentum changes early on and improve your chances of getting the setup as soon as it appears. Candlesticks employ numerous special terms to describe patterns, and I will very briefly define a few of these for you.

All technical analysis involves recognizing change as it occurs, and hopefully, in time, to make a move before everyone else realizes what is going on. This is where pattern recognition becomes valuable.

FIGURE 3.8 - Candlestick Concepts - COGs

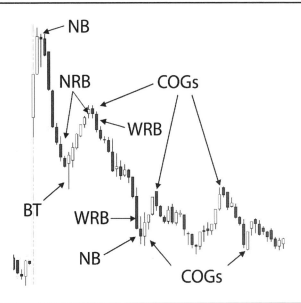

Examples of COGs in downward chart pattern:
Dark Cloud Cover, Piercing Pattern, Bullish Engulfing, Bearish Engulfing, Counter Attack Lines, Thrusting Lines
For color charts go to www. traderslibrary.com/TLEcorner

The candlestick, described as having a counter attack line, can be bullish or bearish, and is simply an opposite reaction of the established trend direction in previous periods.

There are many additional descriptive terms for candlestick patterns, and they are all telling you the same range of information: momentum is increasing or decreasing, range is widening or narrowing and the possibility of change is growing as a pattern develops. It is not useful or necessary to know the various names to increase your under-

Candlestick Patterns

Dark Cloud Cover—a bearish reversal sign. At the end of an up-trend, a long white candlestick precedes a long black one opening higher than the previous day's high. The current black candlestick closes well within the preceding up candlestick's real body.

Piercing Pattern—a bullish signal in which a long black candlestick precedes a lower gap in the next period. The current candlestick moves upward and pierces more than half of the previous period's real body.

Engulfing Pattern—on the bullish side, demonstrates that buying pressure overtakes selling pressure, and is seen by a long, upward, real body "engulfing" the previous small downward real body. On the bearish side, selling pressure is dominant and the opposite occurs: a long downward candlestick fully engulfs a previous small upward candlestick.

Thrusting Line Pattern—can also be either bullish or bearish. The bullish thrusting line is an upward-moving candlestick closing within the range of the previous period's downward real body, without moving higher. The bearish version is a downward-moving candlestick closing within the prior upward real body without moving below.

standing of how trends develop; however, with intra-day trading the candlestick is most practical as a visualization of a more generalized COG concept—trends end and the direction of price reverses. You always look for entry and exit setups, no matter what names you give them.

The narrow range bodies and bars you see are also associated with some specific candlestick names, and this range of patterns is shown in Figure 3.9.

FIGURE 3.9 - Narrow Range Bodies & Bars

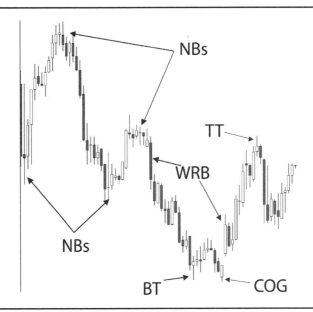

Narrow Range Bodies & Bars: Long Legged Doji Hangman, Inverted Hammer, Shooting Star, Hangman, Harami, DOJI

For color charts go to www. traderslibrary.com/TLEcorner

Narrowing range bodies and bars come in many shapes and sizes. As you see the candle bodies start to narrow, it tells you that momentum is slowing. You want to take note of the trend. The shadows of the candlesticks imply that there is a lot of indecision at these points, but the bodies tell you it is time to start thinking about the potential for prices to begin moving back in the other direction. Some of the popular formation names of narrow range candlesticks follow.

Narrow Range Candlesticks

Long Legged Doji—characterized by exceptionally long upper and lower shadows and opening and closing prices virtually unchanged; the candle looks like a cross. This pattern is typical of uncertainty and volatility in the stock's price, with a lot of price movement during the period. It is difficult to tell in this pattern whether the bulls or the bears will come out ahead.

Inverted Hammer—a bullish pattern containing a very long upper shadow and a small real body. It serves as a reversal signal at the bottom of a downtrendand is a bearish pattern

Shooting Star—a bearish pattern, with a long upper shadow and little or no lower shadow.

Hangman—(or, hanging man) a bearish candlestick with a very small body moving in either direction and appears during an uptrend, anticipating a reversal.

Hamari—is either bullish or bearish, depending on the direction of the current trend. The pattern involves candlesticks over two periods; the most recent pattern demonstrates an exceptionally small real body after a previous day with a large real body, signaling the conclusion of the current trend.

Doji—a pattern with very little real body; the open and close are close together or identical. An upper or lower shadow (or both) implies a lot about setups, and the doji may be thought of as the ultimate narrow range day.

The candlestick is a valuable visual tool essential to intra-day trading. It reveals a lot about price. When you combine candlesticks with moving averages, your insights are even more powerful. The next chapter explains the significance of moving averages.

Self-test questions

1. Candlesticks display current price trends in:

   a. exactly three periods.

   b. less than three periods.

   c. three to five periods or more.

   d. the specific width of upper or lower shadows.

2. A period of price "congestion" is:

   a. exhibited when candlestick bodies cover 20% or more of the same price range as previous periods.

   b. a sign of price uncertainty.

   c. a time when neither bulls or bears are in charge.

   d. all of the above.

3. A "changing of the guard" means:

   a. the bulls are in charge and the bears cannot take over control.

   b. the bears are in charge and the bulls cannot take over control.

   c. the price trend has shifted from one side to the other.

   d. volume has risen, creating a buy setup.

4. An NRB is a:

   a. narrow range bar, often seen at the end of the existing trend.

   b. normal retracement buy signal, expected to appear following three to five down periods.

   c. nominal reaction barometer, an important technical indicator signaling continuation of the current price trend.

   d. neutral rating box, the price range in which neither buyers or sellers are in control.

5. The topping tail is:

   a. a sign that an extended downtrend has come to an end.

   b. a pattern seen at the end of a price run-up.

   c. seen when prices were lower on the period, with a series of diminishing upper shadows over three to five days.

   d. a sign that demand has forced prices into the higher bar segment.

For answers, go to www.traderslibrary.com/TLEcorner

Chapter 4

Moving Average Concepts: Smoothing Out the Trend

Moving averages are the most powerful analytical tools you will find. They keep you focused on where you need to look: at price and not just at indicators. By looking at two moving averages together, you can uncover all you need to know, and ignore virtually all other indicators.

To fully appreciate what moving averages provide, I will demonstrate the power of moving averages in several areas, as summarized in Figure 4.1.

The relationship between separate moving averages, and between the averages and a stock's price, work to provide overbought or oversold conditions. This means that the averages themselves and the trend directions and convergences can anticipate what you are likely to spot using price by itself.

FIGURE 4.1 -An Overbought/Oversold Indicator

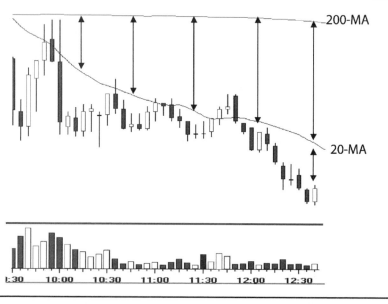

- As the 20- and 200- MAs move farther apart, the odds of a reversal increase.
- As prices move farther away from the 20-MA, odds of a reversal increase.

For color charts go to www. traderslibrary.com/TLEcorner

As you see moving averages begin to diverge, that trend can also serve as a bullish/bearish indicator, again anticipating price. This is based on the technical observation that price movement and strength or weakness is not solitary and does not develop in single trading sessions; it acts within a longer-term trend, which is displayed by those same moving averages.

Moving averages also guide you in identifying emerging support and resistance levels. Most people understand support and resistance in terms of today's top and bottom price ranges; in fact, a range is a distance in price levels that may actually be developing into a more subtle uptrend or downtrend. In those cases, the size of the price range may remain unchanged, but price levels gradually trend up and down. By observing how price interacts with moving averages, you can spot this trend.

> Moving average analysis is effective when you compare trends between the averages, and convergences between the averages and the price.

The moving average analysis also strengthens your ability to spot and anticipate when price reversals are going to occur. Most day and swing traders isolate their analysis to price trends and candlesticks, and this is a valid and effective methodology. However, when you add in the moving average trends and spot how distances are closing or opening in the trend itself, your insight about price tendencies is vastly improved.

The moving average trend is also going to serve as a risk-reward indicator. By this, I mean that some stocks are very predictable and others are very volatile. When you look at price and moving averages together, you can more readily determine that risk (volatility). Some stocks are quite stable but may experience a one- or two-day volatile period; other highly volatile stocks may quiet down for a period of time. In the moment, these trends are very difficult to understand, especially increased volatility. Moving average analysis in the context of price trends makes more sense out of these short-term movements.

Finally, the study of moving averages can be used as a relative strength indicator. Whenever you are looking for a stock's strength or weakness, it makes perfect sense to compare one stock to another. For example, a narrow gap between a 200-period moving average and the stock's price is a sign of strength when compared to a wider gap in the same trends of another stock. In comparison, a wider gap between price and the 20-period moving average is stronger than a narrow gap in another stock. Comparative analysis will invariably improve your insights about both of the stocks you are analyzing.

> To improve moving average analysis, compare the trends not only for a single stock, but between two or more stocks. By making this a relative strength indicator, you vastly improve your ability to spot opportunities.

An Overbought/Oversold Indicator

We will begin with a few specific illustrations of the overbought/ oversold concept. Figure 4.1 shows a basic pattern in which the 200-period moving average (200-MA) and the 20-period moving average (20-MA) are moving apart.

You will notice that the two moving averages are trending farther apart, as shown by the size of the arrows. The farther apart the two averages move, the greater the likelihood of a reversal. In this

FIGURE 4.2 - An Overbought/Oversold Indicator

The relationship between MAs and/or The relationship between Price and MAs Serve as:

• An Overbought / Oversold Indicator

• A Bullish / Bearish Divergence Indicator

• A Guide to price Support & Resistance

• A Tool to help anticipate where a reversal may occur

• A Risk – Reward Indicator

• A Relative Strength Indicator

situation—where the stock's price is in a downtrend—the fact that the 200-MA remains high indicates that the price is going to turn around quite soon. The stock is oversold in this case. The reversal is going to occur, and the gap between the 200-MA and the 20-MA strongly indicates this.

You obtain an additional, secondary indicator by observing the growing gap between the 20-MA and the current price. As this increases, the potential for reversal grows stronger.

This example is indicating a reversal is near because the price trend has been downward and has become extended. However, the same rules apply when prices are moving upward and the averages are located below the price levels. The increase in gaps between the two moving averages and between the 20-MA and price in the current uptrend demonstrates the likelihood of price weakness and, therefore, a downward reversal.

> The simple observation of moving averages above or below current price levels can be revealing and helps you to quickly identify whether the current trend is bullish or bearish.

A Momentum or Bullish/Bearish Divergence Indicator

Figure 4.3 demonstrates a momentum divergence and a COG (changing of the guard) pattern.

In this situation, you find a bullish divergence in the form of a small gap between the 20-MA and price. Note that the gap between these two narrows toward the end of the chart. When combined with a new low, this pattern reveals a slowing in downward momentum and divergence, foreshadowing a reversal and, in this situation, a price rise.

The COG occurs when buyers take over from sellers, or when sellers take over from buyers. This pattern is bullish, as the trend occurs as part of a downtrend; the same observation works in an uptrend. In that case, you will see the 20-MA and 200-MA below current price trend and a narrowing of price with the 20-MA. As that occurs, it signals the end of the uptrend is nearing and a reversal is about to occur.

FIGURE 4.3 - A Momentum or Bullish/Bearish Divergence Indicator

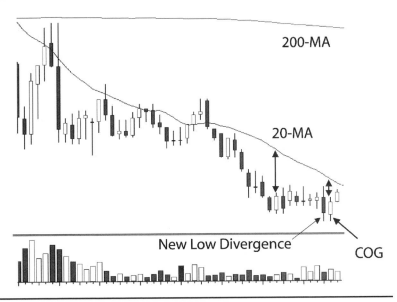

A COG after a new high or new low accompanied by a smaller distance between price and the 20-MA signals a slowing in Momentum and a Divergence.

For color charts go to www. traderslibrary.com/TLEcorner

The momentum indicator is an excellent confirming tool in your analysis. For example, note that at about 10 periods before the narrowing range, you see a NRD after three very clear down days. After seeing this, the swing trading rule labels this a setup. How-

As the price begins to narrow with the 20-MA and 200-MA, it signals the coming end of the current trend. This is important information for anyone trying to time either entry or exit.

ever, the next two days continue in a downtrend, so the setup is contradicted. Then, approximately seven periods of unclear trend ensue. You would look for a confirming signal of some kind after this. The normal three- to five-period setup doesn't take place, but the momentum indicator based on a 20-MA and the price is just as strong. It confirms what the downtrend showed in the previous candlesticks. When you see that congestion pattern developing, you have no idea whether the stock is going to rise or fall; this is where the moving average momentum trends become valuable.

A Guide to Support and Resistance

An additional concept that provides valuable insight involves a guide to support and resistance. The importance of support and resistance as guidance to the moving averages, rather than moving averages actually being support and resistance, is probably one of the biggest discoveries in my search for finding the "truth" in technical analysis. All books and educational material will tell you that moving averages are or should be used as points of support and resistance. I found that this is not the truth.

 Strengthen your understanding of support and resistance with further instruction in the online video at www.traderslibrary.com/TLECorner.

I know this flies in the face of the accepted use of moving averages, but when you consider this in a logical way, you realize that the concept of moving averages being support and resistance is flawed.

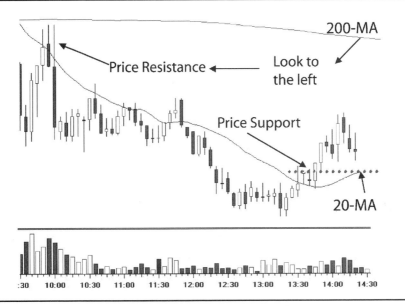

Looking to the left of an MA should point toward an area of support or resistance. A Moving Avg. is a tool that helps the trader anticipate where to enter positions or take profits.

For color charts go to www. traderslibrary.com/TLEcorner

Why? Because, if you have the choice of deciding which moving average to use or what type, that choice will move the location of support or resistance. Common sense tells you that if an area is support, you should not be able to move it. Moving averages should only be used as a guide.

> As valuable as moving average analysis is for studying current trends, you really only need a 20-MA and 200-MA to be effective. If you add too many additional lines to your chart, you do not improve the analysis.

Figure 4.4 provides an example of this. As prices pulled back to the 20-MA it was aligned with the price support to the left. The 200-MA above was aligned with the price resistance to the left. If those moving averages were not aligned with price support and resistance, they would not be reference points that I would use as points to enter or exit a position.

Many traders use moving averages, many as crossover signals, which leads to the question; what length moving averages will give the correct signals? The answer is none, since market environments change and as they do, you get changing price movements. Then consider traders who use moving averages as a specific point where price should stop and reverse. A moving average is just a line on your chart that is providing a visual aid to speed the analysis of price direction, that's all. Support and resistance cannot be moved, but the conventional interpretation of that based on moving averages will suggest just that.

Traders will start by deciding, "Maybe I'll use the 20-MA, or a 30, or the 40-MA," whichever they heard that's the right one. But then maybe it's the 50-MA that should be used or the exponential type rather than the simple type. Can you see how this leads to trader confusion? That's a poor way to perform analysis because the outcome is never going to be reliable. It's this subjective, misleading type of analysis (thinking) that causes so many to fail at technical-based trading.

The reality is that a moving average should really guide you to the actual support and resistance, not be support and resistance. It

FIGURE 4.5 - Anticipate Entry/Exit and Risk/Reward

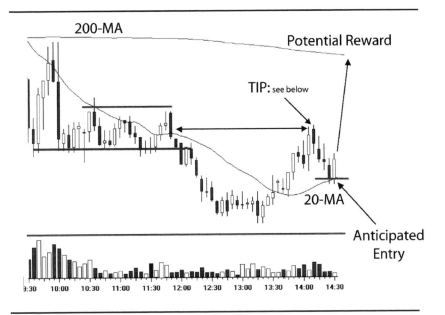

TIP: The correction from the first point of resistance increases the odds that this point will be overcome.

For color charts go to www. traderslibrary.com/TLEcorner

will help you clarify trends and speed up your analysis, but when you look to the left of a moving average, you can identify the point where prices have the potential to change direction. That is, after all, what moving averages focus on.

The moving average is also a tool that helps you anticipate where to take positions. So as I look at my moving averages, if I see my 20-MA following a congestion area, it makes me think that this is potentially where this particular stock or index may change direction. Note on Figure 4.4 how the 20-MA moves down through the price range at the end of congestion.

Price resistance is found at the far left, where the 200-MA clearly sets the top price level. Support occurs at the bottom where the 20-MA scoops beneath the price level and sets the actual bottom. Note that support does not develop through previous price levels alone; for example, you find on the left half a clear bottom in price levels. But at that point, the 20-MA remains above the price levels. It is not until later, near the end of the chart, that the 20-MA provides you with the true price support level.

> To find real support or resistance levels, always focus on the moving average to the immediately left of the current price. That's how you fine-tune your timing for entry and exit.

Anticipate Entry/Exit and Risk/Reward

Support and resistance levels help you anticipate when and where the actual setup occurs and aids you in timing your decisions better. Finding the entry/exit must involve checking these levels, and the key is found in proximity between moving averages and price. Figure 4.5 demonstrates this.

Always look to the left of price and observe the moving average to find actual support or resistance points. It's going to help you anticipate entry and exit points and risk/reward. The entry point is found at the very end of the chart, following the correction from the first point of resistance. Note the horizontal arrow showing these two points; by the pattern in the price and the trend of the two MAs, you can see that this second rise is likely to be overcome.

The distance between moving averages defines potential reward levels. In other words, you can interpret this pattern by assuming that the 200-MA is a future price potential level, and, by the same argument, that your risk is found below the point where COG occurs. These observations also work in reverse. If you were to flip these patterns, the entry/exit and risk/reward would also flip and take the opposite points.

In the pattern of Figure 4.5, note the lowest point is an area of congestion covering about 10 periods. Because the price has been falling down from its previous trading area, meaning sellers have pushed price down, the current congestion becomes very significant. Because the congestion appears, sellers could push prices even lower; but, when you look at the moving average trends, this is unlikely. Note that the 200-MA remains above the action, and the 20-MA pulled down near the congestion, narrowing into the price. This is a bullish sign implying that congestion is more likely to be followed by an uptrend. Moving averages are visual aids suggesting what is likely to happen. The defining moment of when sellers lost control is when the breakdown under consolidation was

Anyone who confines their analysis to a single stock is likely to make errors. By using moving average as a relative strength indicator, you spot additional opportunities and you reduce risk.

immediately followed by a move above it. This type of breakdown failure often precedes the trend reversal.

If we were using a 50-period or a 100-period MA, you could be sure they would be above current prices. You don't need to put while those different moving averages on the chart. That would not add additional useful information. Some of you may be tempted to use too many moving averages, which can lead to confusion. Remember, moving averages are not support and resistance, and it's the price action that we're actually focused on.

FIGURE 4.6 - A Relative Strength Indicator

Comparing the MAs of a stock or index to another will tell us which is stronger. For color charts go to www. traderslibrary.com/TLEcorner

The moving average helps you think ahead of the crowd. Note also that at the end of Figure 4.5, "anticipated entry" is the same as the setup. Seeing the development in the 20-MA, you have a clearer idea about when to enter. Your information is based on price patterns and moving average patterns, not just one or the other.

A Relative Strength Indicator

The final concept involving moving averages is how they work as relative strength indicators. Figure 4.6 compares stronger and weaker trends side by side.

As a relative strength indicator, the moving averages of a stock become very revealing when compared to another stock. As with all analysis, the process reveals more when you do this type of comparison, rather than isolating your view to a single stock.

What should you do when you determine the relative strength of a stock? Comparison provides you with much stronger information and valuation than you will ever find by isolating analysis to the stock price and moving average alone. You can expand on this observation by comparing a single stock to its sector, or to another stock in the same sector. However, some relative strength indicators don't really give you anything of value. For example, when you compare two stocks in different sectors, the variables could make relative strength too subjective to be of any real value. The criteria for "strength" or "weakness" are not valid within the comparison. This is why I encourage you to limit the test of relative strength to the two primary areas: stock to stock within the same sector, or stock to sector-wide.

In Figure 4.6 we look at the relationship between the moving averages and price. A stock is stronger when the gap between price and a 200-MA is narrow. If you look at the beginning of each side of this two-sided chart, you will see what I mean. The stronger stock's price is very close to the 200-MA, and the same gap is wider on the right side, making it weaker. This is one form of comparison. Now, if you had two stocks, both of which have some gap at this point, the stronger of the two would be the one with the smallest amount of distance.

The distance between price and the 20-MA implies the opposite. When the gap between price and the 20-MA is wide, that is a stronger indicator; when the gap is narrow, it is weak. On the left, the 20-MA defines support as price moves upward strongly. The wider 20-MA shows you that the current price is stronger than its prior 20-period trend. When this is narrow, you can conclude that there is little or no room for sustained price growth.

These comparisons are estimates of momentum, used in your quest for the COG or entry/exit. But being keenly aware of gaps between price and moving average is a key to your analysis. It reveals the strength or weakness of the price trend, which is where the gaps between price and moving average become important. Just by looking at the relationship of the prices and the two moving averages, you are very quickly going to see which ones are stronger.

You can see whether that particular stock is over-performing or under-performing in the market.

We have covered six ways of using moving averages to interpret price movement. They are all meant to help speed up the analysis that we can actually do without them. That said, during the trading day analysis must be done quickly; you will make trading decisions in a few seconds. Moving averages are powerful visual aids that help us do just that.

In the next chapter, I will show you how retracement concepts augment your trend analysis. Moving averages are great indicators when studied in comparison to price. Retracement quantifies the strength or weakness of the trend itself.

 The more information you have, the stronger trade you can make. Learn more from the online video at www.traderslibrary.com/TLECorner.

Self-test questions

1. A stock is likely to be in an oversold condition when:

   a. it is moving in a downtrend and the 200-MA is tracking the price closely.

   b. it is in a downtrend and the 200-MA remains high.

   c. both the 200-MA and the 20-MA are higher than the current price.

   d. both the 200-MA and the 20-MA are lower than the current price.

2. A bullish divergence indicator exists when:

   a. the gap between the 200-MA and price narrows over several periods.

   b. the gap between the 200-MA and price broadens over several periods.

   c. the 200-MA and 20-MA both fall.

   d. the 200-MA and the 20-MA are trending in opposite directions.

3. Support and resistance are:

    a. the highest and lowest point in both the 200-MA and the 20-MA.
    b. most likely found when the 200-MA and 20-MA reside at approximately the same price level.
    c. the highest and lowest price points in a stock's trading range.
    d. useful primarily for identifying periods of price congestion.

4. Potential reward levels are found:

    a. in the distance between price and resistance level.
    b. when prices are high and the both the 200-MA and 20-MA are moving up.
    c. when price and both the 200-MA and 20-MA are moving down.
    d. in the distance between the 200-MA and the 20-MA.

5. A relative strength indicator is:

    a. the strength or weakness of a stock in comparison to another stock or in comparison to an entire sector.
    b. indicated by the trends in support or resistance over time.
    c. best applied to stocks in two dissimilar sectors to avoid misleading, cyclical trends affecting the price.
    d. a test of price volatility but not of likely price movements or trends.

For answers, go to www.traderslibrary.com/TLEcorner

Chapter 5

Retracement Concepts: Quantifying Strength or Weakness

The retracement concept is a specific, quantifying system for measuring price movements. It is sometimes referred to as the Fibonacci method, which is an attempt to technically correlate and predict prices based on a mathematical trend.

Rather than trying to use retracement in this way, it makes more sense to get away from the Fibonacci precision measurements, and to use price trends in five specific ways. These are summarized in Figure 5.1.

The first way to use price trends is to measure the strength or weakness of a price move counter to the prevailing trend. This is a key feature in retracement. You are constantly faced with the problem of interpreting contrary trends. Prices move in one direction and, subsequently, they turn. How do you know whether it is a false

FIGURE 5.1 - Retracements Concepts

- Retracement levels are used to measure the STRENGTH or WEAK-NESS of a move Counter to the Prevailing trend.

- The Retracement levels are a percentage measurement between significant highs and lows.

- The Retracement levels we are concerned with are 40, 50 and 60%

- Retracement levels alone are not enough to consider entering a position. A Pristine setup is also needed.

- Learn to see retracement levels without drawing them. When trading, analysis must be done quickly.

signal or a new, strong trend and a true change in direction? If you can make that decision, you can truly profit from improved market timing, not only by the day, but even by the hour or minute.

Retracement is best viewed in levels that are a percentage of change between significant highs and lows. I look for levels which are 40, 50, or 60%, and I will show you exactly what I mean by this later in this chapter.

It's important to keep your eye on the whole picture; no indicator, retracement included, can give you the whole timing picture. You also need a Pristine setup to make your timing work well. I will also

It is never enough to simply track movement of price; you also need to understand the strength or weakness of the trend and its reversals. Your ability to interpret contrary trends defines your trading abilities.

show you how to identify retracement levels without the need to draw them because, in a fast-moving market, you have to be able to do your analysis quickly.

Initially, as part of a learning curve, it makes sense to draw out retracement levels, just to become familiar with them. When you go through the process of learning how to use the tool just by measuring it out, you will become comfortable with it. In time, you will be able to readily visualize where the trend line breaks are. You will not need to actually go out and draw the trend line once you get familiar with how it works.

When you see that a particular stock has moved up or down by a significant amount, eventually you will not need to take out this tool and measure it to see if it's 40, 50, or 60%. Visually, you will know very quickly how important that move is just by glancing at it. Of course, you will need to act quickly when you are trading intra-day.

In Figure 5.2, you will see what a 40% retracement looks like.

Following a 40% retracement, I still consider the trend positive. It will normally continue in the same direction, meaning that the retracement is not a reversal. This applies whether the established

FIGURE 5.2 - Levels and Interpretations

40%

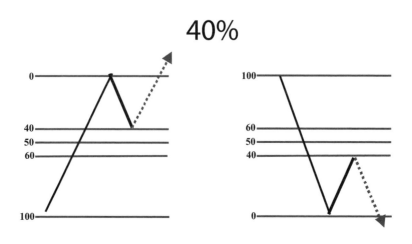

After a 40% Retracement, the trend is still considered positive. The trend should continue in the original direction.

For color charts go to www. traderslibrary.com/TLEcorner

trend is up or down. To calculate the percentage move, you take the highest or lowest price in the trend and calculate the percentage of change. For example, in an uptrend, if the movement went from $30 per share up to $40, you would count $30 as the 100% level and $40 as the zero point. So, a four-point decline would represent 40%. In other words, $40 - $30 = 10 points, and a decline of four points equals a 40% retracement.

> A 40% retracement is positive for the prevailing trend, and, as long as the retracement stops there, you can usually rely on a return to the primary direction of movement.

The same rule applies as part of a downtrend. For example, a stock's price begins at $55 and declines to $50, a drop of five points. The high of $55 is the 100% point and the most recent low of $50 per share is the zero point. The difference is five points, so a 40% retracement would be two points (5 x 40%). In this down trend, if the stock were to rally from $50 up to $52, that is a 40% retracement. Based on the estimate that a 40% retracement does not mean a change in direction, you would expect the downtrend to continue.

Now, let's consider a 50% retracement where the observation is somewhat different. Figure 5.3 shows this scenario.

In this case, the retracement is still considered positive to neutral ("positive" meaning the established trend direction is expected to continue). It is a matter of degrees; whereas 40% is strongly indicative of a continuation trend (with the retracement not a sign of a new direction, but a pause in the trend), 50% is somewhat weaker.

In calculating the 50% level, consider the start-to-finish of the established trend as 100% down to zero percent. The reversal takes back one-half, or 50% of the trend. For example, in an uptrend, a

> A 50% retracement is at the outside border of "positive" and perhaps entering into neutral. This means that you cannot know what is likely to happen next. As a result, your risk increases.

FIGURE 5.3 - "Levels and Interpretations" / 50%

50%

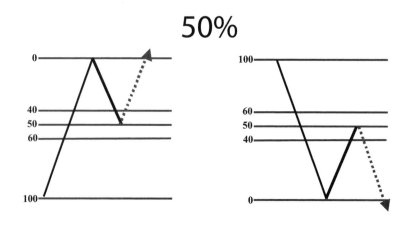

After a 50% Retracement, the trend is considered positive to neutral. The trend should continue in the original direction.

stock rises from $80 to $86, and then retraces back to $83; that is a 50% retracement. On a downtrend, a stock falls from a high of $22 down to $18 (four points), and then rallies back to $20 per share; again, this is a 50% retracement. The implication is that the downtrend is probably going to continue, but it is not as strong an indicator as the 40% level.

Now, I want to show you a 60% retracement level in Figure 5.4.

The 60% retracement is neutral to negative. In this application, "negative" refers to the likelihood of a trend reversal, whether an

FIGURE 5.4 - "Levels and Interpretations" / 60%

60%

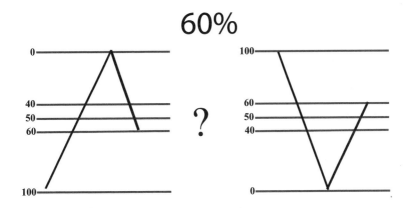

After a 60 % retracement, the trend is considered neutral to negative. The trend is in question.

uptrend or a downtrend. At this point, I start to question what is happening with the stock. The trend is in question, and the possibility arises that the retracement could foreshadow the removal of the previous low (in an uptrend) or high (in a downtrend).

To calculate, the same rule applies. The uptrend starts out at a low, considered 100%, with its high at zero. A downtrend is calculated with 100% at the top and zero at the bottom. In an uptrend, if a stock rises five points and then takes back three, that is 60%. On a downtrend, if a stock falls 10 points and then rises by six, it is also a 60% retracement. In each case, the reversal of direction is substantial, so you have to consider the possibility that the trend has ended, and a reversal is taking place.

If you look at Figure 5.5, you will see a 5-minute chart showing how the 60% retracement level can be interpreted.

This chart shows a rapidly rising price trend with progressive retracement levels, from 40 to 50, and then to 60%. Point A shows the beginning of a retracement pattern; however, is it an entry point? That should be your question. If you had been following this stock and looking for an entry, the ideal point is not found as long as the stock is falling. In fact, as the retracement percentage grows, it tells you to wait out the trend to see what is going to happen next. Now, returning to the standard setup that day and swing traders use, point B provides a standard entry point. There are five consecutive down periods, followed by an up period, and then a narrow range. Now you are in a reversal.

> When are you in a reversal rather than a retracement? The higher your retracement percentage, the greater the possibility that the trend has changed direction.

After point B, you expect to see stabilization and a move higher. This confirms the candlestick pattern indicating a bottom. Now you see the retracement moving in the opposite direction, from 40 to 50, and then to 60%. As the reversal trend tops out, you find a series of congestion periods. At that point, you are not sure what will happen next. However, if you recognized the retracement sig-

FIGURE 5.5 - "Retracement Concepts" / "5-Min."

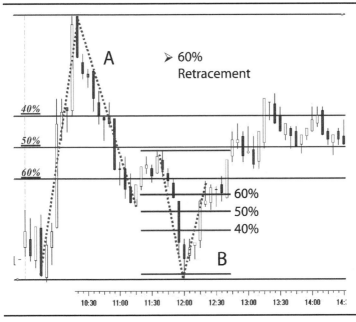

5- Minute Chart

A: Retraced rally by more than 60% (Weakness); expect a move lower.
B: Retraced decline by more than 60% (Strength); expect stabilization and/or a
   move higher.

For color charts go to www. traderslibrary.com/TLEcorner

nals on both trends, you would have been able to play entry and
exit points at both A and B.

Note the bottom of the first retracement, about halfway between
A and B. At that bottom, many traders would expect the price to
turn around, but that did not happen. It continued to go lower. In
fact, those candlesticks for the six periods just before the first low

Retracement Concepts | 93

point do not provide a setup, so this indicates that the downtrend has not ended. Even as the price continued to fall below the 60% retracement level, it made sense to wait out the trend. This is a good example of how retracement can be used to confirm a pattern and seek an entry or exit point. That does not occur until the B level, where the five down periods are followed by an up period and a narrow range pattern. That is the buy signal, confirmed by the developed retracement.

How do you interpret retracement above 60%? In Figure 5-5, there is an example of this. At the very bottom, the price retreated to the 100% level. Now, look at Figure 5.6 for an explanation at this extreme retracement level.

Once a retracement moves to 80% or 100%, it is considered very, very negative (again, in this context, "negative" for the trend, meaning a reversal is almost certain). Now, given the shape of the 100% retracement, this could also be treated as a double bottom or a double top, a classic technical pattern.

These are common patterns, to be sure. Even though the potential is there to continue in the opposite direction, these are negative patterns. The chart on the left, the inverted V, could move higher. In fact, you could expect a short-term rally or, in the case of the chart on the right, a pullback. This is normally the case because

> A double top or bottom, as a technical signal, may confirm what retracement is telling you. Remember, it often means price is going to make a big move in the opposite direction.

FIGURE 5.6 - "Levels and Interpretations" / 80 - 100%

80% - 100%

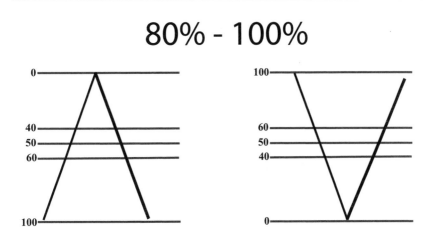

After and 80%-100% retracements, the trend is considered negative. Watch for a double top or double bottom if a COG forms. Expect a short-term rally/pullback

For color charts go to www. traderslibrary.com/TLEcorner

buyers and sellers are continually trading off. As prices fall, buyers make entry; as prices rise, sellers take profits.

If you are going to buy at a potential double bottom, you have to realize you're dealing with a negative pattern. The same is true on the upside. You need to look at these patterns, not so much as simple retracement percentages, but as potential technical signs, testing support (at the bottom) or resistance (at the top) and what that means. A double top or bottom that does not break through often precedes a big run in the opposite direction.

When retracement exceeds 100%, you have to ask whether it is still a retracement at all, or a breakthrough above resistance or below support. In those instances, it may be a fact that a true reversal has occurred, and not a retracement. Analyze the patterns on Figure 5.7.

Here, you see examples of a downward retracement taking out support and an upward retracement taking out resistance. These patterns are negative for the trend and a set-up for the high probability of a reversal. Why? Because, again, buyers look for bargain low

FIGURE 5.7 - "Levels and Interpretations" / >100%

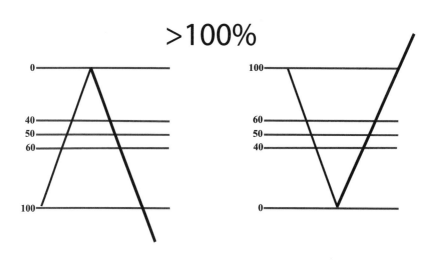

A retracement of over 100% takes out support or resistance and is considered negative, but often sets up a high probability reversal.

For color charts go to www. traderslibrary.com/TLEcorner

prices, and sellers look for profit-taking opportunities. Once price exceeds the trading range borders, those conditions are in effect.

The key to look for is the V pattern because it is not a sign of congestion. The reversal pattern on the left takes out the low and often sets up a retracement back up again. It takes out the stops as the price moves. The same is true for the rise above resistance; so, often, this occurs at a new day's high. It takes out the prior high, which may in fact be a swing high, but it is also a potential point where prices turn back in the other direction.

As to the timeframe for these developments, you will see these emerging patterns in all kinds of charts. I prefer tracking the 15-minute chart for reliable development retracement patterns. That enables me to act quickly while having enough development time for the patterns to show up reliably.

Figure 5.8 gives you an example of a retracement pattern at 100%.

This 100% retracement is decidedly negative. Essentially, it takes back the entire trend and, often, continues moving opposite the previous direction. By definition, a 100% retracement may in fact be a reversal that has simply not been recognized by the active trader.

A 100% retracement is in effect a wiping out of the previous trend, at least for the moment. You need to rely on moving averages and candlestick patterns to interpret the meaning behind such a severe move.

FIGURE 5.8 - Retracement Concepts

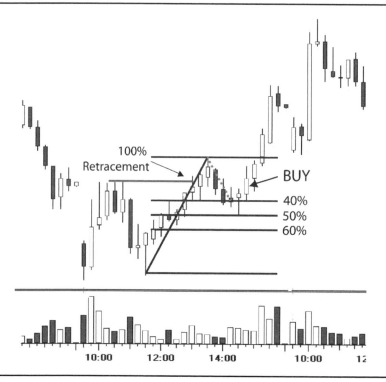

Retracements greater than 100% negate the prior trend. They often set up a high probability reversal point. A move above a prior high signal strength, but is a high risk entry. Buying shallow pullbacks of 40% to 50% after a COG is low risk, professional trading.

For color charts go to www. traderslibrary.com/TLEcorner

Even so, the 100% retracement can also provide you with a very strong reversal signal. For this reason, such an extreme move is very important for intra-day traders. In fact, to know whether or not to make an entry following this kind of move, you need a strong counter-indicator like the one shown in Figure 5.8.

One thing to point out is a 100% retracement clearly negates the prior trend. However, such a move often sets a high probability for reversal (of the retracement). A word of caution: a move above a prior high price is a signal of strength, but it is also a high risk entry. The volatility in this situation cannot be ignored. It offers you fast potential for profit or loss. Finally, buying on shallow price pullbacks of 40% to 50% following a COG is low risk trading, a mark of the professional.

The details of Figure 5.8 prove these points. A strong down trend led to a double bottom and then a 100% retracement. This pattern is very common. After the double bottom, testing support without breaking through, the price rises and moves back in the other direction. The 100% retracement is significant because it leads to another classic pattern: the downtrending candlestick ending with narrow range periods and a big move upward. That is the point at which you want to buy.

 Learn how to identify this point with help from the online video at www.traderslibrary.com/TLECorner.

Look at the volume as well. Volume levels are often quite revealing in these volatile price situations. You saw a peak in volume at the first test of support, and another double peak as the prices came back strongly. This chart shows you that tracking retracement patterns, along with the three- to five-period candlestick patterns, can anticipate price direction and short-term trends quite effectively.

If you're a momentum style trader, you may enter at the obvious reversal points; but, with all trading, you really do not know which direction the price will move. With such high-risk situations, you will want to augment your entry points with stop loss orders, limited capital exposure, and careful monitoring of a developing trend.

> The higher the risk to a particular trade, the more you need to adopt a defensive stance. Use stop orders, limit your capital exposure, and monitor changes closely to avoid losses.

The purpose to all of this analysis is never to ensure 100% profitability, but to improve your odds. Even so, if you ignore the rules concerning risk levels, you will suffer losses you're not prepared for. So, you must be aware of when you are in a high-risk situation.

The kind of retracement pattern in Figure 5.8 tells me that there is strength under these price movements. Volume trends do not have to be perfectly predictable for me to time my entry, but I do like to compare volume to price trends to pick up on that underlying strength. After all, no one wants to trade in weak stocks. From a risk point of view, high profit potential has to be accompanied with a degree of volatility, so I want to see volume matching price movement. I expect to see volume increase whenever the stock makes a big move in either direction. When you see a stock's price move around and there is little or no change in volume, that tells me market interest is poor, and it indicates a lack of price strength.

The kind of pullback you see with these volatile price movements also indicates that, even with the price falling at the beginning of the chart, a lot of traders are not looking for an exit point. They think the price is going to move back up and, in this example, they would have been correct. The pullback is not extreme or long-term, so the changing of the guard (the upward change after the decline from the 100% retracement) is going to be my action point. That is where I see the best chances for a strong movement in the same direction. With this signal, I am going to make a move, whether volume supports that trend or not. In this example, volume more than doubled, which certainly confirms my timing and belief in the direction the price is going to take. That is encouraging, but not essential.

 What is essential? Find out more at www.traderslibrary.com/TLECorner.

The retracement modeling in these examples is valuable information for intra-day trading. In the next chapter, I will expand on this idea with an examination of support and resistance. By defining the current trading range and the significance of the trend, these concepts will help you to become an extremely effective intra-day trader.

Self-test questions

1. The retracement concept involves:

    a. the degree to which a stock's price moves counter to the previously established direction of price movement in the sector.

    b. the degree to which a stock's price moves counter to the previously established direction of price movement in the overall market.

    c. the degree to which a stock's price moves counter to the previously established direction of price movement in the stock.

    d. any of the above.

2. A 40% retracement is:

    a. a positive trend.
    b. a negative trend.
    c. a neutral trend.
    d. a sign that the previously established trend was weak.

3. A 50% retracement is:

    a. a positive trend.
    b. a positive to neutral trend.
    c. a neutral to negative trend.
    d. a negative trend.

4. An 80% to 100% retracement is:

   a. a positive trend.
   b. a positive to neutral trend.
   c. a neutral to negative trend.
   d. a negative trend.

5. A 60% retracement is:

   a. a positive trend.
   b. a positive to neutral trend.
   c. a neutral to negative trend.
   d. a negative trend.

For answers, go to www.traderslibrary.com/TLEcorner

Chapter 6

Support and Resistance Concepts: A Realistic Analysis

The problem with support and resistance is that it is often understood in rather simple terms. While it is true that these features define the top and bottom of a stock's trading range, there is more to it.

You should approach support and resistance analysis with two points of view: actual and subjective. It will help to improve your ability to anticipate reversal of price, which is really what analysis is designed to do. Figure 6.1 summarizes the major points of support and resistance.

Actual support and resistance includes three specific attributes. First, price bars show actual movement of prices, trends, and a defined trading range. Second, prior high and low price levels establish a base for support and resistance, a means for measuring all

FIGURE 6.1 - Support and Resistance Concepts

Actual Support and Resistance:

They are guides as to where traders may anticipate a reversal.

- A series of price bars.

- Prior highs / lows / bases.

- An unfilled gap between price bars.

Subjective Support and Resistance:

Also guides to anticipate reversal points. Without price points in the same area, these are less significant.

- Moving Averages

- Retracements

- Time

future changes. In fact, this is how you establish order within price trends and how you determine when a future movement is significant. It is the testing of support and resistance or exceeding those levels that define what is going on. Finally, you look for unfilled gaps between price bars; gaps become important signs for technical traders because they signal that something important is happening. The actual attributes of support and resistance work as guides as to where you should anticipate price reversals.

On the subjective side, you also look for three attributes. First are moving averages, those revealing 20-MA and 200-MA lines that give you a context for price movement. As you observe how moving averages change and how prices move toward or away from

> Actual support and resistance includes the specific patterns of price: price bars, prior high and low price levels, and unfilled gaps.

them, you begin to develop a keen sense of what is happening in the price trend. Second, retracements are revealing because they enable you to quantify support and resistance. When the retracement stops at a specific percentage, you can determine the strength of the established trend; and, when retracement tests (or exceeds) either support or resistance, you get a very good idea of what is going to follow. Finally, time is an element that you can use to make sound conclusions. The rate at which trends develop or reverse can be very telling, because acceleration of a trend or retracement indicates that momentum—that all-important feature of price—is changing as well. These subjective features are excellent guides for anticipating reversal points. The subjective points have to be viewed in context; this is why you always want to check to the left of the moving average to identify support or resistance.

In Figure 6.2, you can see an example of unfilled gap resistance on a chart.

Note the gap itself at the beginning of the chart. The gap, or course, is a point where distance exists between closing at one period and opening at another. The gap established resistance when it went

> Subjective support and resistance involves timing and trends beyond price from one period to the next, representing trends: moving averages, retracements, and time.

FIGURE 6.2 - Support and Resistance Concepts

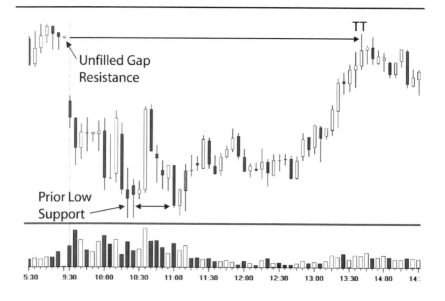

- Anticipate sellers in the area of Unfilled Gap
- Anticipate buyers in the area of Prior Low Support

For color charts go to www. traderslibrary.com/TLEcorner

unfilled. This is what you should be thinking when you see prices coming into an unfilled gap. You should expect to see sellers in that area. At the far right of the top, you then see a topping tail (TT). This pattern tests the gap resistance and confirms that we should now anticipate that sellers are going to be moving in, especially after a move up like the one shown on the chart. To summarize, in this example the unfilled gap sets up a form of resistance, and the prices fall. After a series of congestion patterns, prices rise all the way up to that gap resistance. The topping tail signals that the sellers are once again about to take over.

This is a good example of how you can combine the use of price pattern recognition with support and resistance. Note that at the prior low point, you see a double bottom. This should tell you that buyers will come in right around this area, and even though the congestion pattern follows, the signal is reliable. If you were to play this swing using both the traditional technical signals (double bottom, for example) and an appreciation for the resistance and support indicators, your timing could be quite accurate. By observing the actual candlestick signals, retracements, and a setup indicating pending reversal, your timing will be vastly improved.

 Check out the video online at www.traderslibrary.com/TLECorner to hone your observation skills.

Next, you will want to think about the idea of resistance forming at a prior base.

Figure 6.3 illustrates this concept with an example of resistance at a prior high. This occurs when a previous support level (bottom) is transformed into a new resistance level (top), which happens when the trading area is broken. Note the unfilled gap support at the very bottom of the steep downward trend. The gap follows another brief downward run ending with a bottom tail. This formation is not only a double bottom, but it occurs in between two interim topping tails. These tests of support and prior high resistance are very strong signals. There are two points to remember. First, you anticipate a reversal in the area of the unfilled gap (in this case, at the bottom). Second, you have to anticipate that sellers will dominate in the area of prior highs. These are classic patterns. Sellers hit the price at or near prior highs, and buyers take over at those lows.

Now, look at the series of eight down days, then the narrow range period, then the gap. This is a clear signal, as clear a signal as you are likely to find that a reversal is occurring. Momentum was strong on the downside, but the price pattern tells you that the downward

FIGURE 6.3 - "Support and Resistance Concepts" / "Prior high resistance"

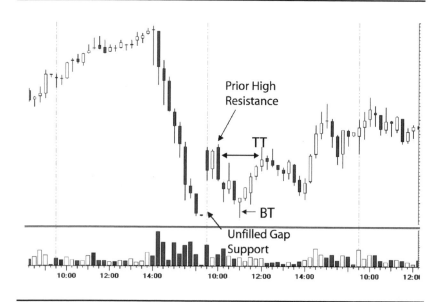

• Anticipate sellers in the area of Prior Highs
• Anticipate a reversal in the area of Unfilled Gap

momentum is slowing, and it is time to take a position. The narrow range is the first strong signal; the gap is the second. Remember, strong momentum in one direction is likely to be followed by equally strong momentum in the other direction, once the reversal occurs. The upward price gap is a very strong reversal signal after an extended price decline. This type of open gap will serve as a reliable focal point of a turn for traders if prices move into that gap.

Another example of these patterns and their predictability can be found in Figure 6.4.

FIGURE 6.4 - "Support and Resistance Concepts" / "Resistance at prior base"

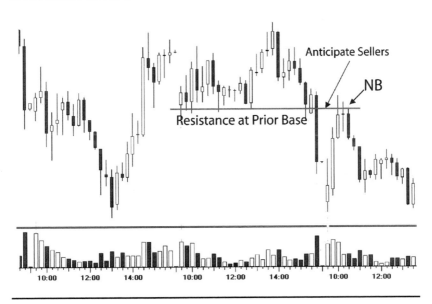

Tip: What was support will become resistance

For color charts go to www. traderslibrary.com/TLEcorner

Think of charts and their interpretation from the mindset of other traders. What are they thinking? Can you anticipate what other sellers and buyers are going to do? Why are price movements strong or weak, and what causes gaps to form? In this situation, a strong price uptrend leads to a new support level, which is equal to the prior base. This simply means the trading range has shifted, at least temporarily. You find the support at the prior high and then, once the price breaks through the support level, you anticipate sellers; of course, the price then drops.

> If you try to look at charts from the mindset of other traders, you can add a type of objectivity to your analysis. Too many traders limit their focus to their own conclusions (and desires), so they do not anticipate reversals as easily.

It is also interesting in this pattern that the short-term price increase, right before the breakout, is an indication of lowering momentum on the buy side. The sellers are in control here, and the newly established support level could not hold.

If you also check volume, you see that buyers were in control for a short period of trading, but volume was far higher once sellers took over. This is yet another confirming sign that momentum has shifted to the sellers.

The next chapter moves beyond the detailed analysis of support and resistance to provide you with some valuable market timing tools. Specific kinds of indicators will help you manage your setup signals so that entry and exit timing will be more accurate.

Self-test questions

1. Actual support and resistance refers to:

   a. price bars, moving averages, and time.
   b. price bars, prior high and low price levels, and unfilled gaps.
   c. moving averages, retracements, and time.
   d. trading range, moving average trends, and volume.

2. Subjective support and resistance refers to:

   a. price bars, moving averages, and time.
   b. price bars, prior high and low price levels, and unfilled gaps.
   c. moving averages, retracements, and time.
   d. trading range, moving average trends, and volume.

3. An unfilled gap is:

   a. a pattern in which a price gap is found between one period's close and the next period's open, without a subsequent price reversal to fill the gap.
   b. a price movement in which a high volume of trading prevents a trader's open orders from being filled in a timely manner.
   c. always a sign of eroding price support or resistance.
   d. a sign that technical information is lacking due to price congestion.

4. Resistance at a prior base is:

   a. a strengthening of a previously established resistance level.
   b. replacement of previous support levels with a new established resistance level.
   c. a simple shift in the trading range.
   d. confirmation of established support level after a double bottom.

5. Checking volume during periods of reversal tells you:

   a. that as the volume changes, the indication is contrary to price direction.
   b. the entry point is imminent.
   c. that price gaps are about to form in the direction of the established trend.
   d. which traders—buyers or sellers—are in control.

For answers, go to www.traderslibrary.com/TLEcorner

Chapter 7
Market Timing Tools: Who Is In Charge?

Market timing is not merely fine-tuning the entry and exit decision. It is so much more. You should never expect to operate at 100%, meaning you buy at absolute low, and sell at absolute high. Two important points worth making here are a) you will do well to approximate entry and exit points based on your analysis; and b) you will succeed in trading by performing better than the average. Market timing is a useful tool for recognizing and anticipating reversal points, based on the indicators and trading patterns you have studied in previous chapters. By adhering to a program that makes sense and requires self-discipline, you will succeed.

You need to perform an on-going level of analysis in a broad sense, simply to know what the overall market is doing. Market sentiment, mood, and strength/weakness move individual stocks, without a doubt. Any day that you see a sharp upward or downward movement of the averages, you will also see a majority of listed stocks follow suit. The Dow Jones Industrial Average (DJIA) contains only 30 stocks but it has significant influence over day-to-day and intra-day pricing of stocks.

> Because the majority of stocks tend to move with the average, you need to watch the broad market; however, you can time entry and exit points based on the action in individual stocks.

This influence cannot be ignored. Remember, in the long term, strong stocks will rise and weak stocks will fall; but, in the immediate moment, you are going to mostly see substantial price movement based on market-wide trends. This is the key to profits in intra-day trading: the recognition of two forces working together. First is the influence of the overall market; second is the series of indicators and trends within each individual stock. The more volatility and the more action within the overall market, the more likely you will see some big moves within a stock and within its intra-day indicators.

A valuable overall indicator to watch is the TRIN indicator. This is an acronym for TRading INdex. It is used to determine who is

> **Quick Bio:** Richard Arms is a financial consultant based in Albuquerque, New Mexico. He won the 1995 Market Technicians Award and has written several books about technical analysis. His TRIN is listed each day in the Wall Street Journal and is considered a key technical indicator.

in control of the market, buyers or sellers. This is also called the Short Term Trading Index and the Arms Indicator, named after its creator, Richard Arms.

The TRIN is a contrarian indicator intended to signal when the market is over-bought or over-sold. A rising TRIN is bearish and a falling TRIN is bullish. The formula for calculating TRIN is:

$$\text{(advancing issues ÷ declining issues)} \div \text{(advancing volume ÷ declining volume)}$$

Figure 7.1 further illustrates the TRIN indicator.

FIGURE 7.1 - "Market Timing Tools" / "The TRIN Indicator"

The Trin Indicator: Used to determine who is in control of the market.
- Readings below 1.0 indicate more volume is entering advancing issues; Buyers are in control
- Readings above 1.0 indicate more volume is entering declining issues; Sellers are in control

For color charts go to www. traderslibrary.com/TLEcorner

When the TRIN reads below 1.0, it indicates that a majority of the current volume is entering advancing issues, and buyers are in control. When the TRIN is above 1.0, it indicates that more volume is going into declining issues, and sellers are in control. The five-minute chart gives you an example of this situation.

> When TRIN rises, it is bearish; when it falls, the sign is bullish. This is a valuable indicator because it combines the number of issues and the trend in volume.

TRIN is a useful confirming indicator, an additional piece of information that you can use to bolster what you are observing elsewhere, or to counter what other indicators mean. The TRIN simply tells you who is in control at the moment, but does not always dictate the direction of price movement into the future. As an inverse indicator, TRIN tells me that when the number is moving up, it may be wise to consider shorting stocks; when it is moving down, I should buy.

> No indicator—including TRIN—tells the entire story. However, this is an excellent confirming indicator that you can use to fine-tune your entry and exit timing.

The example of a declining TRIN in Figure 7.1 shows little change in price. In fact, the trading range is quite thin, and there is very little movement. In a situation like this, I would be inclined to recognize the congestion and the growing weakness from the TRIN and look for price dips. That would be the time to buy. Remember, a weak TRIN indicates market strength. When you see a shift in

FIGURE 7.2 - "Market Timing Tools" / "The TICK Indicator"

The TICK Indicator: Used to determine Market strength and directional changes.

- Readings above 0 indicate more stocks trading on upticks, favors longs.
- Readings below 0 indicate more stocks trading on downticks, favors shorts.
- Prior highs and lows are used as points of support and resistance in the broad market.
- + 1000 indicates excessive buying; odds of a reversal are very high.
- - 1000 indicates excessive selling; odds of a reversal are very high.

For color charts go to www. traderslibrary.com/TLEcorner

the prices and in the TRIN, it is a strong indication that momentum is shifting.

Another interesting market timing tool is the TICK indicator. Figure 7.2 provides further explanation.

Tick is used to determine market strength and to anticipate change of direction. It is computed as the net difference between all uptick and all downtick issues at any given point during the day. So, if an equal number of stocks rise and fall at the same time, the TICK indicator would be zero. Online tracking is available for NYSE, AMEX, and NASDAQ. The NASDAQ is probably going to be more volatile than the NYSE because of the mix of issues. Most days the direction for TICK will be the same on all exchanges, but their respective levels will most likely be different.

> The TICK is merely the difference between the number of rising and falling issues, and it reveals market strength at any specific moment. It also anticipates reversals.

The TICK simply tells you who is running the course of the market at this moment. If there are more upticks than down, it is bullish; if the TICK indicator is minus, meaning there are more down issues, this situation favors going short.

Another point to remember is this: when the TICK is greater than +1,000, it indicates excessive buying, and the odds of a reversal are going to be very high. On the downside, the same caveat applies. When the TICK indicator exceeds -1,000, there is excessive selling, and the odds of an upward reversal are high.

> Any directional indicator may reach a point where the implication reverses. As TICK exceeds 1,000 in either direction, the chances for a reversal increase.

With the TICK, I like to use prior highs and lows as points of support and resistance in the broad market. This indicator is telling me how many stocks are trading on upticks versus downticks. At a prior point, where it turned back down, the majority of stocks at that time in this area were trading on upticks. From this, I can identify broad market resistance and support as shown in the chart. If stocks are trading outside of these market ranges, it reveals a great deal. When a TICK indicator for the broad market is compared to an individual stock's performance, you can better judge its buying or selling strength.

The TRIN and TICK are simply overall estimates of market conditions. This means they may conflict with one another at times and, when they do, I would give greater weight to the TRIN because it encompasses more: advancing issues, declining issues, and volume. You might have a situation where TRIN is rising above one, then stocks start to bounce in the opposite direction and the TICK starts to move higher. Overall, TRIN tells you where most stocks are heading during the day. As the TICK moves up, I would be inclined to stay on the sidelines and look for short setup opportunities; however, that is secondary to what I see in the TRIN.

> TRIN and TICK are not always going to be in agreement. When this occurs, you should give greater weight to TRIN because it includes calculation of the volume trend.

In Figure 7.2, the negative area that is trading below the dotted line indicating zero, shows you when and where to expect trading to swing back up. The same is true above the zero level; when the point of broad market resistance is met, the likelihood is that prices are going to trend back down toward the middle. It's a matter of degrees. I focus on that 1,000 level, recognizing that when the trend exceeds such an imbalance in either direction, it is a strong reversal signal—usually. However, in extreme cases, you could see TICK exceed 1,500 or even 2,000. On exceptional bull or bear periods, that can and does occur. The 1,000 level is not a magic, automatic point to make an entry; it is only one of many indicators.

In the next and final chapter, I will summarize the major points for you, thereby fitting these theories into a neat package.

 Listen and learn from all of Capra's theories presented in this book with the online video presented at www.traderslibrary.com/TLECorner.

Self-test questions

1. TRIN is an acronym for:

   a. Trading Range Indicator Number.

   b. Trading INdex.

   c. Top Range Influence Negative.

   d. Total Resistance Implied Neutrality.

2. TRIN is an indicator that:

   a. determines who is in charge, buyers or sellers.

   b. is also called the Arms Index.

   c. is also called the Short Term Trading Index.

   d. all of the above.

3. A rising TRIN is:

   a. bullish.

   b. bearish.

   c. not reliable as a directional indicator.

   d. applicable only to volume.

4. The TICK indicator:

    a. is the sum of all uptick and downtick issues, divided by 1,000.
    b. should be at or near zero in a healthy, balanced market.
    c. determines market strength and anticipates changes of direction.
    d. tracks only NASDAQ issues.

5. TICK is computed by:

    a. subtracting the number of downtick issues from the number of uptick issues.
    b. subtracting the number of uptick issues from the number of downtick issues.
    c. dividing the number of downtick issues by the number of uptick issues.
    d. multiplying the net difference between uptick and downtick issues by 1,000.

For answers, go to www.traderslibrary.com/TLEcorner

Chapter 8
Putting It All Together

Even though our focus here is on very short time spans of trading, I recommend that you always begin by observing a longer time-frame. This is your guide to the trend of the market and to each individual stock. All of the indicators I have provided in past chapters can and should be used in conjunction to create and employ an effective method for recognizing and anticipating signals, fine-tuning entry and exit, and making your moves before the market crowd sees what you see.

> Intra-day trading relies on short-term chart periods. However, the longer time frame is also valuable because it shows you how trends are developing over time.

FIGURE 8.1 - Putting It All Together

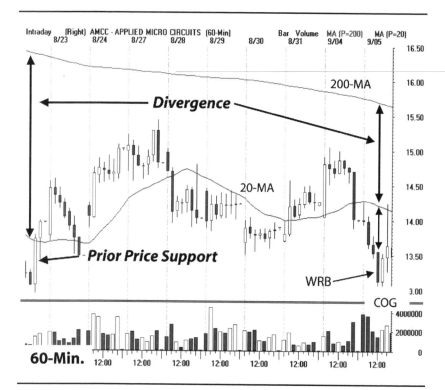

Start with the longer time frame

For color charts go to www. traderslibrary.com/TLEcorner

Start With The Longer Time Frame

Let's examine what Figure 8.1 shows you. This is a 60-minute chart covering nine trading days. Although a lot of specific patterns are going to show up on 5-minute and 15-minute charts, you can still get a broad view of a stock. In this case, Applied Micro Circuits

(AMCC) traded during this period from an initial low of about $13.00 up to $15.50 per share.

The longer time frame (in this case, a matter of days) enables you to observe price, moving averages, and a series of potential entry and exit points.

Always keep an eye on the traditional indicators, such as tests of price support and resistance. A test that does not break through often results in strong movement in the opposite direction.

Prices Test Support

It is revealing to observe how price trends test support in a volatile situation, even over a few trading periods. Figure 8-1 starts out with a test such as this. Note the extreme distance between the low price test level and the 200-MA.

Over the period of this chart, a couple of additional forays near support occur without breaking through, until the very end of the chart period.

 A WRB is an exceptionally strong signal. It represents a lot of price action on the period, a sign that the direction of price movement within the WRB is gaining momentum. Learn to recognize the WRB with the online video at www.traderslibrary.com/TLECorner.

Be Alert For The WRB!

At the very end of the chart, note the wide range body that has formed. This is a strong entry signal. Why? First, draw your attention once more to both the 200-MA and the 20-MA. The 20-MA has been weaving through the price range throughout this chart, as you would expect. Even though the 200-MA has declined slightly, it remains strongly above the trading range and the 20-MA.

In addition, the WRB comes right after seven previous days of downtrend, and it rests right at support. If this chart ended at this point, the signal would be there to buy. The next two days perform just as I would expect, rising strongly. Note the topping pattern on the last trading day, with trades reaching far above the closing price level.

A COG Signals the Decline is Over

This changing of the guard pattern tells you that the decline is over. The price is very likely to begin moving upward from this point forward. You not only have the candlestick patterns in support of

A COG is not a random event. As sellers and buyers switch positions, the trend changes as well, especially when you also find confirmation through other indicators.

this contention, you also have the 200-MA and 20-MA patterns. In the 20-MA, you see virtually no deterioration of the pattern, and the 200-MA has declined only slightly. Momentum during the downtrend has now decreased, signaling that, once again, the downtrend is coming to an end.

In other words, this COG is strongly confirmed by additional indicators. The traditional technical observation of this pattern could even point to a double test of support (at the beginning and end of the chart). Remember, we call this chart a longer time frame, but for those traders looking at daily charts, it covers only nine periods. So even with all of the action taking place here, this is a double bottom pattern. Other confirmation is found in all of the remaining chart features.

Moving Average Divergence

Another feature of Figure 8.1 is the trend between the two moving averages. At the beginning of the chart, a huge gap exists between the 200-MA and the 20-MA. But over nine days, that gap has been cut in half. The divergence is reducing over time and, based on this pattern, I would expect to see this continue as the price rises.

When this occurs (reduced divergence or, more accurately, convergence), it serves as a confirming attribute of the current trend. Keep in mind what these two moving averages represent. A 200-MA and a 20-MA are moving closer together, meaning reduced volatility, closer price tracking, and a further sign that the downtrend has ended.

> Short-term price trends often have more to do with the overall market strength or weakness, momentum, and sentiment than with a company's fundamental strength. This is why you should always check the market..

Check The Market and Look for Entry

The advantage of this longer time frame is that it strengthens your overall analysis. An individual stock will rise and fall based on both technical and fundamental news; but, no matter what is taking place in the fundamentals, stocks are going to react to market trends as well.

With this in mind, you will also need to check our two market-wide indicators, the TRIN and the TICK. Figure 8.2 summarizes the TRIN once more.

> **Key Point:** Remember, TRIN is an inverse indicator. A positive TRIN is bearish, whereas a negative is bullish. The pace of change in TRIN gives you a good idea of what comes next.

FIGURE 8.2 - "Putting It All Together" / "The TRIN indicator"

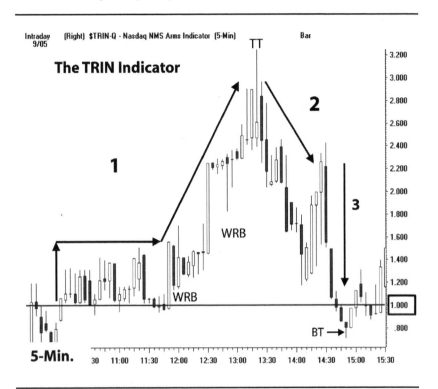

The TRIN Indicator

Intraday 9/05 (Right) $TRIN-Q - Nasdaq NMS Arms Indicator (5-Min) Bar

5-Min.

1. Trin above 1.0 and Rising. Sellers are in control.
2. Trin above 1.0 but Declining. Sellers are losing control.
3. Buyers taking control, note angle.

For color charts go to www. traderslibrary.com/TLEcorner

This is an example of the NASDAQ Arms Indicator (TRIN) on a five-minute chart. Early in the day (1) you see the indicator rising and ultimately reaching an extreme level. Sellers were in control in this situation. Note the recurring wide range bodies on the way up.

Although this is a market-wide index, you need to interpret the candlestick patterns in the same way you would on an individual stock. Because TRIN is an inverse indicator, the wide range bodies leading to the topping tail (TT) tell you that sellers are in control. At the top, momentum rapidly shifts, and the numbers begin moving downward.

FIGURE 8.3 - "Putting It All Together" / "The TICK indicator"

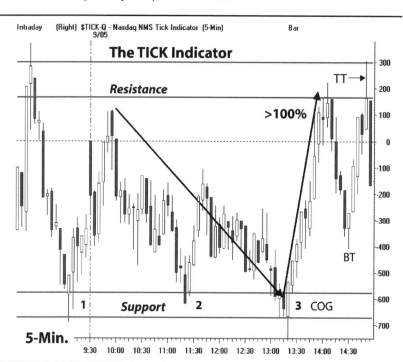

Triple Bottom: A> 100% retracement into resistance signals strength. Look to buy the pullback. TICK enters the Broad Market Resistance Area. Expect Momentum to stall.

For color charts go to www. traderslibrary.com/TLEcorner

At the trend declines, sellers start losing control (2). The indicator is still above 1, but it is deteriorating. This drop tells you there is a shift underway, and that selling momentum is rapidly falling. As the trend reaches a bottom (3), the buyers take control. The TRIN has reversed, and the rapid fall signals a long entry. Note the angle on the drop. It is so steep that the signal is clear. The bottom tail is a strong signal, especially following these very large reversal bars. Buyer momentum is coming in at this low point, which is also prior price support and an important support test.

> Use TICK to figure out who is in charge and track changes in the TICK indicator to spot increased or decreased momentum. This helps you identify a likely COG way ahead of the market.

The TRIN, in any moment in time, tells you very little; however, when you observe the trend in Figure 8.2, you can see that the direction and speed of price change is revealing. The rapid momentum on the downside at (3) clearly signals the end of the downtrend and anticipates a strong reversal.

You also want to keep the TICK indicator in mind, as shown on Figure 8.3.

This five-minute chart shows a lot of important movement in the TICK. The fast decline in the previous day's prices comes into a sharp decline. Looking at the two days together, this is a triple bottom. A double bottom is invariably a good technical sign that prices are going to rise; but a triple bottom is even stronger, an almost certain signal that a rally is going to follow.

FIGURE 8.4 - "Putting It All Together" / "Oversold MAs wide"

Intraday 9/05 (Right) AMCC - APPLIED MICRO CIRCUITS (5-Min) Bar Volume MA (P=200) MA (P=20)

Oversold MAs Wide. Deep Retracement above the 20-MA. After a PBS, BUY!
Target 200-MA Price Resistance. Offer at Resistance. TT 60-Min. is Bearish.

For color charts go to www. traderslibrary.com/TLEcorner

This pattern also includes retracement over 100%. This is a sign
that a significant amount of strength is coming into the market
and, therefore, prices will rise. Whenever this extreme occurs, you
have to expect a pullback. This occurs down to a bottoming tail,
and then a secondary rally takes the level on right to the topping
tail. The TICK was able to come into an area of resistance and

> Trend anticipation is always the key to effective entry and exit. By employing a combination of reliable indicators, you can become adept at finding the best entry and exit points.

take out a prior high in a straight upward move. After a V bottom, these kinds of strong movements are significant. It signals exceptional strength.

The triple bottom signals a strong changing of the guard. Even so, you have to expect momentum to stall, which explains the pullback. In this situation, I would look for the bottoming tail and buy right after that pullback. This pattern indicates a very strong upward trend.

You will also observe that when the TICK is entering broad market resistance, momentum is going to stall. That's a good time to exit. Check Figure 8.4 to see how this applies in the case of Applied Micro Circuits.

In this situation, you can see that moving averages diverged while retracement exceeded 60%. Also note that the topping tail point is a second test of resistance, which works as a sell signal. I'd be inclined to exit after that run-up—especially as I observe the 200-MA and 20-MA converging. That convergence is not extreme, but you always want to anticipate the price trend.

 For further explanation, check out the video online at www.traderslibrary.com/TLECorner.

FIGURE 8.5 - "Putting It All Together" / shows four smaller charts

For color charts go to www. traderslibrary.com/TLEcorner

There are several things happening in Figure 8.4 right at or near the top besides the moving average trend. First, you have a wide range body on the upside, the fourth of five uptrend periods. That last uptrend is a narrow range period with the topping tail. If you consider the clear candlestick pattern, the WRB and the NR with TT all together, this is a very, very clear exit signal, especially following such a large retracement and double test of resistance.

Remember, think ahead and anticipate what other traders are going to do in the situation. Once this stock gets up into the topping area and the selling starts, you can offer out your stock all the way back down. The odds of you being taken on the offer become less and less because now the momentum has shifted to the downside. If you've missed the boat by offering out your stock into resistance, you should just be hitting the bid at or near the clearly signaled top. That is going to be your best action at that time.

In a nutshell, these are the main points of intra-day trading:

Candlesticks are excellent tools for quickly identifying the movement within a single period and recognizing important technical patterns such as bottoming and topping tails, wide range and narrow range periods, and sequential upward or downward patterns.

Moving averages provide good overviews of direction through a period of time even when interim trading is quite chaotic. As the 200-MA and 20-MA converge or diverge, you receive additional indicators. The proximity between averages and price is also valuable information that helps you anticipate what will happen next.

Support and resistance are the structure of a trading range. As these levels are tested, you gain knowledge about whether those levels will hold, and what price direction is likely to follow, especially with familiar patterns like double top and bottom, triple, and head and shoulders. When gaps form around breakthrough at support or resistance, you have a strong indication of a new rally (on the top) or decline (at support).

TRIN and TICK are great market-wide tools for developing an understanding of who is in control. When your stock is holding steady or rising, but the overall market is being controlled by sellers, you need to proceed with caution. Eventually, your stock can be dragged along with the crowd. These are also great confirmation tools, especially when momentum, is picking up or slowing down.

Momentum determines who controls price, and when you see it slowly, anticipates changes and reversals. This is a great entry and exit tool because it is invariably right. If you see momentum slowing, expect a change in the immediate future.

COG (Changing of the Guard) is the expression of changed momentum, the action of a trend ending and a reversal beginning. When sellers are in control, it eventually leads to a COG; when buyers are in control, the same rule applies. The one thing you can be sure of about the current trend is that it is going to change.

Finally, I recommend that you try and look at several indicators at the same time. Figure 8.5 provides a good overview of the concepts.

Always remember that you will time entry and exit better by using a limited number of highly informative signals. If you try to use too many, you clutter up your charts without improving information. If you use too few indicators, you lack confirmation and may end up responding to false signals.

An excess of indicators distorts analysis without improving the quality of information. Too few indicators robs you of confirming information. You need an efficient, accurate balance.

The range of concepts I have explained in this course book were designed to give you the best level of information in most situations. As a final reminder, I suggest that when in doubt, do not put money at risk. If signals are contradictory, it probably means a period of congestion is evolving, which also means you have no reliable way to anticipate the next important move. You will never achieve 100% accuracy in the timing of your trades; but, if you can get as high as 70 or 75%, you will be doing quite well for yourself and will have mastered the tactics of intra-day trading.

 Become a master intra-day trader with Greg Capra's help from his video presentation online at www.traderslibrary.com/TLECorner.

Self-test questions

1. A longer time frame for chart analysis is:

   a. contrary to the rapid requirements of intra-day trading.

   b. less reliable than the 5-minute and 15-minute chart.

   c. enables you to observe what is going on with a clearer view of a stock's trend.

   d. useful for big-cap company stocks but not for smaller companies or for market indices.

2. WRB stands for:

   a. widening resistance band.

   b. weak retracement bottom.

   c. wide range body.

   d. weekly recap balance.

3. A COG tells you that:

   a. the previous trend is coming to an end.

   b. the previous trend is confirmed and will continue.

   c. the previous trend is uncertain as you enter a period of congestion.

   d. a degree of moving average divergence is occurring.

4. In studying the 200-MA and 20-MA, remember that:

   a. the two averages are unrelated.

   b. divergence between the two is a meaningful signal.

   c. only the 20-MA has any significance when compared to price.

   d. in addition to these two, you also need to use a 30-MA.

5. TICK and TRIN are:

   a. market-wide indices.

   b. relevant only in uptrend markets.

   c. unreliable for judging whether buyers or sellers are in charge.

   d. the same indicators, but with different names.

For answers, go to www.traderslibrary.com/TLEcorner

Trading Resource Guide

RECOMMENDED READING

PROVEN CANDLESTICK PATTERNS
by Steve Palmquist

Currently one the most widely used chart types, candles have the potential to be an effective tool for extracting profits from the market. But with all of the information out now about candles, how can you tell which ones work and which don't? After testing every known candlestick pattern, Steve Palmquist has determined which candlesticks are the most effective and gives you extensive data and techniques for how to best incorporate them into your trading strategy.

Palmquist's extensive back testing has revealed :

· How effective popular candlestick patterns such as Bullish Engulfing, Bearish Engulfing, Hammers, Hanging Man, Evening Star, and Morning Star really are,

· Actual data on these popular candlestick patterns in different market environments to confirm when they are most effective at predicting winning trades,

· Which of the three major market environments to successfully use specific candlestick patterns -- and which environments to avoid,

· How to use the massive information collected to truly confirm various candle patterns and eliminate the guess work.

Steve Palmquist's new 90-minute course arms you with what you need to know about candlestick patterns and shows you the candlesticks you should be using and which ones you should avoid. Don't spend years collecting this powerful information and definitely don't let another day go by without using the proven power of these candlestick patterns!

Item #5197576 - $99.00

STRATEGIES FOR PROFITING WITH JAPANESE CANDLESTICK CHARTS
by Steve Nison

What are Japanese Candlesticks and why should traders use them? This brand new video workshop will help you understand and master this powerful tool with high impact results. Steve Nison is the premiere expert on Candlesticks in the world and now you can benefit from his expertise in the comfort of your own home. Filmed at a unique one-day seminar he gave for a select group of traders you'll find discover -The Most Import Candle Patterns -Using the Power of Candles for Online Trading -Combining western technical indicators with CandleStick Charts for increased profits -Reducing risk with Candlestick Charts -Swing & Day Trading with Candlestick Charts and so much more. It's an incredible opportunity to have the foremost expert guide you to trading success now at a great savings. Also available in VHS version.

Item #2434165 - $695.00

21 CANDLESTICKS EVERY TRADER SHOULD KNOW
by Dr. Melvin Pasternak

There are 100 candles patterns with which traders should be familiar and 21 candles they should know by name. Knowing their names allows traders to spot them more easily and assess their implications. When faced with the need for a quick decision during the heat of trading, the trader who can name these 21 candles has a distinct advantage over the one who can't.

Item #4050479 - $19.95

SWING TRADING SIMPLIFIED
by Larry D. Spears

Learn the basics - or refine your swing trading skills - with this swing trading primer. With a foreword by the popular "MrSwing.com" - Spears makes the powerful Swing Trading concepts more accessible and easy to implement than ever. Now at a great introductory price.

Item #1674501 - $29.95

TOOLS AND TACTICS FOR THE MASTER DAYTRADER: BATTLE-TESTED TECHNIQUES FOR DAY, SWING, AND POSITION TRADERS 1ST EDITION
by Greg Capra and Oliver Velez

A no-nonsense, straight-shooting guide from the founder of Pristine. com, designed for active, self-directed traders. Provides potent trading strategies, technical skills, intuitive insights on discipline, psychology and winning methods for capturing more winning trades, more often.

Item #11221 - $55.00

To get the current lowest price on any item listed
Go to www.traderslibrary.com

This book, along with other books, is available at discounts that make it realistic to provide it as a gift to your customers, clients, and staff. For more information on these long lasting, cost effective premiums, please call us at (800) 272-2855 or you may email us at sales@traderslibrary.com.